PEARLS

Published by Newhouse Books
Copyright © 2013 By Fawn Germer, Second Edition
Library of Congress Control Number: 2011913761

Some contents of this book were originally published
in *Hard Won Wisdom* (Perigee 2001),
    Mustang Sallies, (Perigee 2004), and
    The NEW Woman Rules, (Network Books 2007).

Design: Ryan Torres, ryantorresdesign.com
Cover: Barbara Willard
Studio Photography: Lisa Presnail, South Tampa Photography,
southtampaphoto.com
Copy Editing: Lynn Stratton and Jayne Bray
Printed in China through Four Colour Print Group, Louisville, Kentucky

PEARLS

Powerful Wisdom from Powerful Women

By Fawn Germer

NEWHOUSE BOOKS

For Mom and Dad
and their true love.

Acknowledgments

People always assume that Oprah's endorsement turned me into a best-selling author. The truth is, my friends did that, weeks before Oprah even saw my book. When *Hard Won Wisdom* came out, members of my gang were joking about a competition to prove who loved me the most by buying the most copies. Miriam Reed bought 25 copies at $25 each at one of my signings. When someone plunks down more than $600 for books just to support you, you know you've got a friend who wants you to win. All of my friends were and are there for me and the true reward for my life's work is not the books themselves, but the friends who supported my dream.

I used to try to name all the people who helped me, but I always forgot somebody who I loved way too much to hurt. I'll just say that I have been blessed with the world's most amazing set of parents, great mentors, the best friends and readers who have partnered with me in a way that has helped us all to grow stronger together. My spirituality has given meaning to this experience. I have so much to be grateful for, and I am. Every minute of every day.

I am so grateful for the women who agreed to be interviewed for my projects. Most of them gladly participated because they are as committed to mentoring other women to succeed as I am. They made me feel strength, and I hope I have passed that on to you.

Finally, thank you for reading my book and joining me in this experience. I wish you love, hope, strength and possibility. Stay in touch. I love hearing from readers.

Fawn Germer
fgermer@fawngermer.com
www.fawngermer.com

Introduction

A dozen years ago, I went looking for a book that would teach me how to lead as a strong woman in a male-dominated environment. I was having serious problems in my job as a newspaper editor and needed help. I couldn't find a single book that told me what to do when I was being undermined and knifed in the back. A friend said, "You're a journalist. Why don't you write it?" As a journalist, I was sick of charlatans writing books on subjects they knew nothing about. But then it hit me: No one had gone to the greatest women of our times and asked them what they'd learned the hard way. As a journalist, I could get to just about anybody. I'd get the mentoring wisdom I so desperately needed, and I could pass on what I learned.

I am forever grateful to the first woman who said yes to me. Former Congresswoman Patricia Schroeder was the first person I asked. She had been my congresswoman when I was a newspaper reporter in Denver, and she quickly scheduled an interview. I remember talking with her about women having an insatiable need to be liked, and she said, "The good thing about politics is that you only have to make 51 percent of the people happy. You don't have to make 100 percent happy." Then came Nobel Laureate Betty Williams, whom I'd befriended when she came to Denver for a lecture. She urged me to dive into the project, saying, "Darlin', how are you ever going to learn to fly if you don't jump off the cliff?" Third, I called Helen Thomas, the dean of the White House press corps. I remember telling her, "I keep getting in trouble and getting told that I don't know my place." Helen was outraged. "What is your place?" she demanded. "It's what you say it is. It's not what they say it is." So began what I now call my "million dollars worth of free therapy."

I've since interviewed presidents and prime ministers, Nobel Laureates, Olympic athletes, generals, CEOs, astronauts, Academy Award winners, and trailblazers such as Hillary Clinton, Martina Navratilova, Ann Richards, Erin Brockovich, Susan Sarandon and others.

There were more than 200 interviews in my first three books, and the words of the sage women changed me in profound ways. They taught me how to bolster self-esteem, take risks, persevere and blaze trails. They've shown how we already have so much power—we just need to use it.

I've made no secret of the fact that my first book and I traveled an obstacle course filled with repeated rejections and setbacks. I think it was called *Hard Won Wisdom* for a reason: It was a depressing and arduous journey that ultimately led me to the highest highs of my life. Once I surmounted my obstacles, I won something far more valuable than I'd ever have gained if it had happened easily. I gained the strength to stand on my own, sure I would succeed–no matter what.

Holding that first book with my name on it would not have meant nearly as much if it had happened simply. I wouldn't have learned how important my friends were in keeping me going when all signs from the universe said to quit. I wouldn't have seen how unconditional the faith of my parents was and is, because as bad as it got, my Mom kept saying, "I know it is going to be a best-seller." If I hadn't had all that time to kill, waiting for something to happen, I never would have found my parallel career as a professional speaker–something I love as much as I love my work as an author. It was a long, hard road, and it led me to true happiness. That's my hard won wisdom.

The words of these great women have made me bolder, happier and more passionate about life. Oceanographer Sylvia Earle inspired me to leave my career as a newspaper editor to dive into the unknown as a full-time author. Columnist Ellen Goodman coached me to persevere when my first book was released the day before September 11. Gen. Claudia Kennedy guided me as I ventured out as a speaker trying to spread the word.

My second book, *Mustang Sallies*, was born when I keynoted for a group of executive women in Arizona. After the speech, one woman told me, "I need your help. I keep getting told I come on too strong and I need to tone it down. They say I need to stop being so aggressive, and I have been called a bitch, and…" The whole time she was talking to me, I kept wondering, "Why are you asking me about that? That's my problem!" Then it hit me: Are other strong women going through that? It was the birth of *Mustang Sallies*.

My third book, *The NEW Woman Rules*, is the book that can most directly impact the careers of my readers. More than 50 of the most powerful women in American business lay out the rules for tracking up the corporate ladder– and doing it fast.

I have long wanted to do a book with my favorite quotes from all of these interviews. We don't always have time to scour a book for the nuggets of wisdom that are meaningful for us. This is the book that makes that wisdom simple and accessible. I keep hearing, "What a great gift book." It is a gift book, but the gift is really from the women who did the interviews so you and I would have an easier path to travel. Dog-ear these pages. Mark them up. Be stronger, because that is what these women intended. They wanted to give you the courage to gain ground for a new generation of trailblazers.

The quotes from *Hard Won Wisdom* and *Mustang Sallies* come first in this book, and the insights from the business women in *The NEW Woman Rules* come later. Sometimes you want to check in for inspiration and motivation, and other times you need serious career mentoring. You don't always need them on the same day, so the front of the book provides the motivation and the back of the book provides the powerful nuts and bolts of success.

A few months ago, I ran across the file with all my rejection letters for *Hard Won Wisdom*. I have no idea what gave me the courage to keep fighting for my dream when there were so many signs that I needed to give up. I had a plan for success, but nothing went according to plan.

I often tell my audiences, "Have a plan! It's the greatest piece of fiction you will ever write." There will be obstacles, but the greatest wisdom in life comes when you detach and see that obstacles are just setbacks—not end points. I don't wish for a journey free of obstacles, I wish for the strength, ingenuity and faith I will need to conquer them and prevail.

You have the strength to get beyond your challenges. It is through your crucible experiences that you will find your power. The things that come easy don't mean much. The things that come hard force us to define who we are.

And the Winner is…

I am constantly asked who gave me my favorite interview, and I always say that if I answer that question, I'll never get another interview. Still, there were a few standout experiences, and this is a great place to kiss and tell.

Biggest life-changer

Kristine Fugal Hughes copped to a self-esteem issue because of her weight problem. Hughes founded Nature's Sunshine Vitamins and, because of her, I asked every woman in *Hard Won Wisdom* about their self-esteem. When I realized our role models have the same insecurities we do, I stopped beating myself up.

Most profound lesson

Brenda Barnes used to be the CEO of Pepsi-Cola North America but left because she wanted time with her family. Once her kids were in college, she went back to work—as CEO of Sara Lee Corporation. She suffered a major stroke and had to step down. Life is so fragile, and her earlier decision to put family first is a real lesson for all of us.

Most arrogant person

An Ivy League professor who was so snooty I haven't included her in this compilation.

Most regular person

Academy Award winner Frances McDormand. Talking to her was like talking to a girlfriend.

Most strategic situation

Getting Hillary Clinton. She'd never have agreed to it if I'd gone the traditional route of requesting an hour. I pounced on her at an event.

Most difficult interview to get

Susan Sarandon. It took multiple routes and numerous requests. Finally, she called me. I was sitting on my couch thinking, "I'm sitting here talking to Susan Sarandon. This can't be real."

Easiest to get

She'll kill me for saying this, but the lovely Ellen Goodman, who actually answered her own phone and agreed to do it on the spot.

Most memorable moment

Having dinner with Helen Thomas, asking her what Eleanor Roosevelt was like, and getting an answer.

Interviews I wanted, but never got

No. 1: Former U.S. Supreme Court Justice Sandra Day O'Connor.

No. 2: Meryl Streep, who I just felt like talking to.

No. 3: Dolly Parton, because I think we would have gotten along great.

Nicest handlers: Wynonna's people. I never did get the interview, but they sure were nice about saying no.

Worst handler

Olympic legend Jackie Joyner-Kersee. Her publicist literally had me
calling two or three times a week. When I didn't have an answer after
more than four months, I figured I wasn't being persistent in trying
so hard; I was being stupid.

Most real

Nobel Laureate Jody Williams, who led the movement against
land mines, for showing that anyone can achieve greatness if they
believe they can, and that you just have to shut up and do the work.

Most natural mentor

Nobel Laureate Betty Williams (no relation to Jody), who knew I
needed support back when I was a reporter and became a long-
distance mentor.

Two who had my back

Sheila Coates and Aida Alvarez, who pushed Oprah's people to get
me an endorsement. A producer was trying to interview them about
their stories from my book, without crediting the book. They insisted,
then Oprah came through—big time.

Most missed

Susan Butcher, four-time Iditarod champion. Reading that she'd died
of leukemia just blew me away. She was so honest, so accessible—
and so alive.

Most validating

Dr. Alexa Canady, who said, "If you are an agent of change, you can't look to the status quo for validation because you will never get it. That's why the status quo is the status quo. It doesn't want to change." This woman—the first African-American woman to be a neurosurgeon—changed my world. Suddenly, I understood why I'd always felt like an outsider.

Rowdiest interview

You should have been there for the Brett Butler interview. Love her. Second prize goes to Carnie Wilson, who is real and funny and real funny.

Surprisingly brilliant

Martina Navratilova. She was absolutely one of the smartest individuals I've ever talked to. We talked politics for quite a while and she was spot-on informed, and voiced original ideas with great perspective.

Most awkward interview

For sure, Janet Reno. I asked about Monica Lewinsky, which she hadn't had to address before, because, as attorney general, she could say she couldn't comment on a pending investigation. This did not endear me to her.

Most exhausting

I tried to interview Japan's most powerful businesswoman by telephone, and we could barely understand one another. I was sitting in my office, gesticulating wildly—as if she could see me and understand me. I ended up dumping the interview.

Best friendship

Gen. Claudia Kennedy, who always gives a great interview. She helped me to get speaking events when I was just starting my business and proved she is a great mentor and friend. She even invited me to her wedding and, let me tell you, that was a wedding.

Most committed to mentoring other women

Almost all of the women. They gave the interviews because they know their true legacy comes by passing on what they learned in order to make others stronger and more determined.

"What separates an **ordinary woman** from an **extraordinary woman**? The belief that she is ordinary."

Jody Williams, 1997 winner of the Nobel Peace Prize for the movement against land mines

"I have engendered a lot of reaction. Some of it is, frankly, who I am, and I brought it on myself. **But some of it came from the expectations people have about women, what women are supposed to look like, do, say, act, et cetera.** What I've tried to do—under some pretty challenging circumstances—is just to be able to go to bed every night feeling like I did the best I could do at being me."

Hillary Clinton

"You can do some crazy things when you believe. Every human being on this earth has a purpose. **Everyone has something they can give.** The need is there and you rise to the need."

Sheila Coates, founder of Black Women United for Action

"If you have a passion, you have to go for it. You have to live that passion. That is what life is about. It's also about challenging yourself. **You have to go for it. If you fall short, you get up and try it again** or figure out another way."

Cammi Granato, former captain of the women's U.S. Olympic Hockey Team

"Nothing comes to you if you just sit there and wait. You have to look for things yourself. I have two mantras. First, 'If you aren't doing something, you're doing nothing.' Second, 'Don't let security be your dangerous anchor.' Some of the things you try won't work. All you say then is, 'Oh, that one didn't work. I'll try something else.' "

Jill Gould, who went to college and then medical school as a mother of five and became one of the nation's first women forensic pathologists.

"It's like a ladder—when you put your hand on one rung and your foot on another, **you ought to be eyeballing something two rungs up**. There is always something else."

Dr. Nancy Dickey, first woman president of the American Medical Association

"I was really lucky to have a really bad first boss. Keep a notebook. Remember how it feels. **There is nothing better than a bad boss to teach you** to be a good boss."

Geraldine Laybourne, founder and former chairman and CEO of Oxygen Network

"When you get done being jealous at the end of the day, what does that give you? It doesn't give you their looks or their talent. Instead of saying, 'Why them, not me?' say, 'Why them? Let me go to work on me.' *Don't attack them.*"

Women's rights activist **Faye Wattleton**

"I had peers who went to the officers' club—who still go to the officers' club—in hopes of marrying an officer. I used to think, 'Good God. Why marry one when you can be one and fly a plane?' "

Paula Coughlin, the ex–U.S. Navy pilot who forever changed the armed forces after she fought back in the Tailhook sexual assaults

"We can influence other people by what we say and what our attitudes are. Even in the most boring job, you can make a difference with your fellow workers, just with your attitude. Every individual matters, has a role to play and makes a difference. **We have this huge collective power—if only we'd use it.** But, we have this great 'me-ism.' You know, 'I'm one person. I live in an expanding world of people. What can I do to make any difference?' It's apathy. What we do makes a difference for the future."

Anthropologist and primatologist **Jane Goodall**

"I have nothing to gain or lose. **Fire me from my job, put me down, do what you want to me.** It's not going to change anything, because if you do or do not like me, fine. I don't frankly care."

Erin Brockovich activist

"I think **having to live with low self-esteem makes you stronger.** Your arsenal of weaponry has to be a little more elaborate."

Academy Award winner **Frances McDormand**

"I was brought up to expect to be treated as equal and to act as equal, as well. **We were encouraged to form our own opinions.** That is very much what led me to be the person who I am today. Quietly confident to believe I am as able as anyone else to lead a country."

Jenny Shipley, former prime minister of New Zealand

"I have a profound sense of inadequacy. I was not brought up to feel good about myself. We have been conditioned to not think of ourselves as achievers. We don't escape the power of that conditioning by success. I was not programmed to think of myself as beautiful or smart or worthy of attention. I always strive to be better and to justify the goodness that people think is in me. **But the self-doubt is there, and I wonder if I am a fraud and if I am as capable as people think.** These are questions that still constantly burden me."

Faye Wattleton, the famous women's rights activist once named by People magazine as one of the twenty-five most beautiful people in the world

"Someone once told me, 'You are such a hard worker.' I answered, 'The truth is, I'm really lazy. Thank God I am brilliant.'"

Former Canadian Prime Minister **Kim Campbell**

"When I would say, 'I'm Gayle Greer,' it wasn't enough to stop. It was, 'I'm Gayle Greer, senior vice president of Time Warner.' One day, you look around and you have all the things you think you should have, and you still aren't there. You don't feel right."

Gayle Greer, who now just says she is Gayle Greer

"Have you ever heard it said that a man has an 'edge'? I can't tell you how many times, during planning or human resource kinds of work, they'd talk about a woman's style and say **she has an 'edge' on her. Compared to whom?** I would look around the room and see a guy who was a total jerk, yet she has an 'edge'? Compared to him, she's a pussycat. But it didn't fit in that range of what they consider acceptable for women."

Caroline Turner, former senior vice president general counsel of Coors Brewing Company

"I had a real fixation with mirrors from the time I was about sixteen. I remember being in a nightclub with a guy I had a crush on and there were mirrors all over the place. He said, 'Do you mind looking at me when I talk?' **I was so scared that the next time I looked, I'd be ugly.** I lacked a sense of identity. . . . When you leave therapy, you don't leave the demons behind. You simply learn how to control them."

Rita Moreno, winner of the Oscar, Emmy, Grammy & Tony awards

"One day, I wondered what I would think if I was somebody at one of my shows watching me perform. I started to realize that, if I wasn't me, **I would like me**. That is such a wonderful thing to realize. That is true power."

Comedienne, **Margaret Cho**

"How you dress says a lot about what you think about yourself. **If you want to be taken seriously, then dress like you take yourself seriously.** Women who come in with a bunch of chains around their neck, earrings dangling off their ears—it tells you something. It tells you that this is a frivolous person. And that you have deliberately adorned yourself in a way to cause a distraction from what you have to say... I want it clear that I'm here to work and I'm here for business. This is not a style show."

The late former governor of Texas, **Ann Richards**

"One of the problems so many women have is, we care what people think about us. That they talk about us. I have had so many bad things said about me, so many innuendoes. It really used to break my heart. Then I got a little tougher and a little tougher and a little tougher. Not that I don't care anymore. **I care, but I don't let it stop me**. Women have yet to learn how to get tough on the inside, how to have a harder shell. That is why it is so important to believe in what you are doing. If you really, truly believe in what you are doing, that gives you a lot of power."

Linda Chavez-Thompson, former executive vice president of the AFL-CIO

"It's a real challenge to be yourself. Obviously, that doesn't mean you can be rude or discourteous and get away with ill behavior, but at the end of the day, **you have to be satisfied about who you are**. Nobody else can live your life."

Hillary Clinton

"Just relax. You may think somebody is in there thinking about you **every minute of every day,** but it ain't happening."

Kathleen Carroll, executive editor of the Associated Press

"We always think we did something wrong. **It's our fault, it's our fault, it's all our fault. You have to step outside of yourself,** see the world through other people's eyes and see some decisions are made that have absolutely nothing to do with whether you are great at what you do or are failing at what you do."

Laura Ingraham, national radio host and author

"There are so many ways in which we are so critical of ourselves. Women will be brought into the emergency room having been in an accident or shot or whatever, and they'll say, 'I'm sorry. I didn't have time to shave my legs this morning.' **We are so quick to criticize ourselves**. We all have those tapes in our heads, critical tapes, and we are the first to know what our faults are. We're always going to have those tapes. The key is to offset them. Make other voices louder."

Sarah Weddington, the attorney who won the landmark 1973 Roe v. Wade case in front of the U.S. Supreme Court.

"Do you want to be the mainstream? I never strived to be average or normal. The mainstream just follows. How can you strive to be there? I was never afraid of leading or speaking out or doing things my way—the way I believed they should be done. **At the end of the day, you have to like yourself**. You have to like what you see in the mirror. Are you living your life for everyone else, or for yourself?"

Tennis legend **Martina Navratilova**

"Never sell your soul because nobody can pay you back. Ever. Being your whole self, your true self, is as much a part of success as anything else. I am who I am. I have my own style and it has freed me to bring my whole person to work. Not only does it make it a lot more fun, but it has helped make me successful. **I sometimes hear people say they are a different person at home than they are at work. I feel bad for them.** The workplace isn't getting who they are. And both the workplace and the person are missing something. If you can't be yourself at work, find a different workplace. If you feel you are constrained or are selling your soul or leaving a part of yourself behind, then you aren't performing to your potential and should go somewhere else."

Carly Fiorina, former CEO of Hewlett-Packard

"When you find yourself in a bad situation, do something. **Do the right thing. Tell the truth.** If you make a mistake, own up to it. I would love to be aside from that and not have been a part of all this personally. When you find yourself in these situations, try to think back to your moral compass and determine what is the right thing to do. There are some gray areas and real ethical dilemmas. But, as hard as it may be, take that first step, then follow through. A lot of people take the path of least resistance. Don't go along with the crowd. Do the right thing."

Coleen Rowley, the FBI whistle-blower who testified to Congress about how the government mishandled intelligence and might have prevented 9/11

"Many people resist risk and are only comfortable with the security of knowing, when they go to sleep at night, what the next day is going to be like. That's comforting. It's secure. And living like that is a choice they are free to make. I recognize the importance most people place on having structure in their lives. Not having structure can be disconcerting. They should not try to do what I do if structure brings them peace and comfort. **Risk is a choice. It is the only way to test your potential.**"

Oceanographer **Sylvia Earle**, "Her Deepness"

"The message I was trying to send wasn't always the message that was being received. You need to do a number of things to make sure—not that people agree or have been persuaded, but that they understand what you mean. **Sometimes, when you are trying to explain what you are looking for, you should explain what you are not looking for.** And ask questions like, 'Does that make sense to you? Does that seem clear?' Do that knowing there are people who won't ask questions in public places or knowing there are people who want to sit with things a little before they ask questions."

Kathleen Carroll, executive editor of the Associated Press

"You have to be able to say, 'This is what I do well and this is what I don't do well.' Bring people in who do what you don't do well. I am not as detail- and process-oriented as would be desirable for a company our size. I have a real clear idea of where we want to go. If we are in San Francisco and we want to go to New York, I know what New York will look like, but not how we'll get there. I don't know that we'll need 16,000 gallons of gas, food, or certain people on the bus. I don't have patience for detail. Our chief operating officer—that is his strong suit. My strength tends to be seeing where we are going, and the courage to get the organization focused on the fact that we are going to get there."

Meg Whitman, the CEO who turned eBay into a way of life

"I think a lot of women are raised to think they have to keep asking for permission to do things. They don't realize that they don't need permission. They can just do it. **It takes a lot of courage to do it because we are raised to ask permission. If you don't take the chance, you don't reap the rewards.** Woody Allen said 80 percent of his success was that he just showed up. Sometimes, by just showing up, you get what you are after. It's having the courage to try it, the courage to take the chance."

Kathrine Switzer, the first woman to officially run the Boston Marathon

"There is this very macho mind-game playing that they do—a lot of lying to each other and bravado. They lie about how their team looks or what their plans are or how they are running their race. They either act cocky like they have a better chance of winning than they actually do or they act really humble when they actually have an incredible chance of winning. I have watched them win using this mind game. I couldn't play it and I finally went to not playing mind games. I just had the best possible team I could have, and I was honest about my chances. **They'd ask a question and I'd be 100 percent truthful. That was confusing to them.** They didn't get my ways any more than I got theirs."

The phenomenal, late **Susan Butcher,** winner of four Iditarod titles

"Anything I do for the first time is scary, whether it is anchoring Nightline or throwing my daughter's wedding. What works for me is to just go do it. I feel that way about life. It isn't worth a lot of agonizing about and it's certainly not worth a lot of planning. These young women who say, 'First I'm going to get married, then get the job, then have the children. . . . Well, probably not. It won't work that way. Life will happen to you. **Things will happen to change your life's view while you are busy planning.** The best thing is to just do it. Get up, put one foot in front of the other and don't be afraid to take new challenges, even if they are scary, because it is going to be interesting. And, you learn something."

Cokie Roberts, ABC News

"You are a part of a team. It is not necessary for you to know everything because **other team members will know pieces you don't.** Figure what you have to contribute, then do it to the best of your ability. Never commit to do something that you do not follow through and do. Your word is your bond. Take responsibility. Be known as reliable."

The late, legendary Texas Governor **Ann Richards**

"I'm one of those people who thinks if you want something enough—really enough—and you are going to work for it, in a lot of cases, it's going to happen. If you have a very strong belief, you can make it work. If there's something that I really want to do, I'll just go and do it. If I don't succeed at something, I'll come back to it."

Singer **Joan Armatrading**

"You have to say what you think, even if you feel it's risky. What's the worst thing that can happen? It's not cancer. That doesn't mean you hit somebody over the head with an ax. **But say what you think so other people can hear it…** You're not going to win the first time out and if you get defeated or if you run off feeling rejected the first time or the second time or the fourteenth time, find another way to do it. Find another way to be persuasive, or find another way around it… Shrillness doesn't work. You have to ask what you want. What is your goal? Do you want to make your point, do you want people to listen to you, or do you want to vent? If you want to vent, go home, get into the shower and scream. If you want to have a public argument in which people will actually listen to you, get a grip. Pay attention to what the other person is saying, and as you are speaking, feel comfortable arguing back. It takes time."

Columnist **Ellen Goodman**

"We have this God-given gift of a woman's intuition, but we don't use it. Eighty percent of all business decisions are made on intuition and 20 percent on analysis. **I always tried to make decisions based on what is for the greater good.** The only time I have ever felt good about anything was if I felt good about it. It's when you know it is good. You don't need some goofy CEO to tell you that it is good."

Geraldine Laybourne, founder, chairman, and CEO of the Oxygen Network

"You have to give people a vision about what can happen, and you have to act as if it can happen and **you have to believe it can happen.** It's acting into the truth."

Marie Wilson, president of The White House Project and former president of the Ms. Foundation

"I got a lot of letters after I was ordained. Most of them were very positive and encouraging, but there were a number from women and men who were angry. They were citing the letters Paul wrote that said women are to keep silent in church, women are not to ask questions in church, and if women want to know something, they should ask their husbands when they get home. **I got letters from people who said they were praying I would change my mind and renege on my vows.** Some men wrote proposing marriage to save me from my predicament. Others wrote that I was a sinner for being ordained. I was overwhelmed. Numb."

Rev. Margaret Towner, the first woman ordained in the Presbyterian Church

"**If you are an agent of change, you can't look to the status quo for validation because you will never get it. That's why the status quo is the status quo.** It doesn't want to change. I find white women have a great deal of difficulty with this—much more than black women. They have always been revered, welcomed, and included in everything. The concept of being someplace where you are not wanted or included is devastating to them. It is the one time that it is better to be black. When you are pushing your way where people don't necessarily want you, you can't expect that they will be supportive of your goals. Your validation has to come from your family, which is the pattern of black America because society never did validate us."

Dr. Alexa Canady, the first African-American woman to become a neurosurgeon

"You can't just walk in and give orders. Find your place. Your place is what you choose it to be. If somebody wants to push you out of your place, stand tough. Be firm. If they don't like the fact that you are where you are, don't even compute that. **Always know where your friends are and where your enemies are.** Know what people think of you, who you can trust. But don't be consumed by it. Keep it in your peripheral vision and focus straight ahead. The most important things that I have done that were lasting and had purpose were the most difficul   t to achieve and the most controversial at the time."

Dr. Bernadine Healy, former director of the National Institutes of Health and president and CEO of the American Red Cross

"If you spend any time with small children where one says, 'He hit me first!' and the other one says, 'No, he hit me first!' you have to get everyone calmed down and distracted by introducing a common project. Management is often like that. **One of the strengths of women is that they think in terms of solving a problem or working together to get things done.** Very often, women are better at bringing people together and stopping the squabbling."

Alice Rivlin, former director of the Office of Management and Budget and former vice-chair of the Federal Reserve System

"The one thing they say about me is that I'm sincere. There's no phoniness. What you see is what you get. In order for this company to grow, we just have to find more people like that. We're not the kind of people who are slick. I really think that one day we are going to be judged. The judge isn't going to say, 'How did you run Nature's Sunshine?' It's going to be, **'How did you treat others?'** I try to be very aware of that."

Kristine Fugal Hughes, who founded the $320 million-a-year Nature's Sunshine Vitamins with $150 and an idea

"I don't think hanging off the handrail of the spaceship in a space suit changes a person's core philosophy or values or spiritual views. I don't think being two hundred miles above the Earth is something that struck me to being closer or farther from the powers that be. I often get that question, 'Up there, do you feel closer to God?' I think you feel closer to God holding the hand of someone in great pain who needs you. I feel closer watching a baby cry. There are thousands of ways. Traveling two hundred miles anywhere doesn't put you farther from or closer to anything."

Kathryn Sullivan, first American woman astronaut to walk in space

"What you say is not always the most important thing. Your willingness to sit and listen is. **Be open and try to learn from every person,** whether they are older or younger, because every person has something to teach."

Rabbi Sally Priesand, the first woman ordained as a rabbi in the United States

"Last night, I had a dream I was back in competition at the Winston Cup, working my way in front of the other drivers. I was competitive. I was right there, not leading, but I was working my way up to the front of a very dense pack. **One driver looked over and said, 'She's back.'** You know how dreams are. They are strange."

Janet Guthrie, the first woman to race the Indianapolis 500

"If you get burned the first time and back away and don't try again, you never move forward. If you do that, how do you grow? I know where the line is and I know there is life after what I am doing. There are other opportunities. **This is not the job that is going to define who I am.** It is a part of my life. It is not who I am. I am so much more than this. You have to make time for the other things in your life."

Yolanda Moses, former president of the American Association for Higher Education

"Don't be content to be in a job that has no path
to where you want to go, because in the long run,
**you're going to be more miserable than if you'd taken
the risk and failed...** It's very important not to settle."

Janet L. Robinson, New York Times CEO

"You have to follow your own instinct and your own voice. My friends were taking normal jobs, and I was doing what was right for me. It might have looked like I was not doing what was safe, but nothing is safe. **You can go to work for a corporation and end up getting laid off.** Just do what you really want to do and don't be afraid."

Carol Higgins Clark, author

"**If you aren't willing to risk losing, you are never going to win.** You've got to be able to face your challenges, even if it means losing. And, sometimes when you think you have lost, you've won. Other people admire the fact that you have taken the challenge, so you've actually had a moral victory."

Aida Alvarez, former head of the Small
Business Administration

"When you realize you have just been short or rude with somebody or somebody says they were worried about something for a whole day, you realize a little of you goes a long way. I hope I never forget and never lose sight of the power of the job. I hope I never lose sight of how important it is to be graceful with that, to never seem too busy to talk to people. **You need to be seen, be in the departments and in the hallways, and remember to say, 'Thank you,' and 'Nice work.'** I don't do enough of that. If I did nothing but that ten hours a day, it wouldn't be enough. But it's always a goal to say, 'Thank you,' and 'Nice job,' more often."

Kathleen Carroll, executive editor of the Associated Press

"Sometimes you are going to wind up working for a bad boss. Assess the situation. Figure out how bad it is, how long it is going to last, and if you can figure out a way to get along with the bad boss in order to get what you really want. A lot of people will go to work for a bad boss and say, 'That's it. I'm out of here.' But, **sometimes, you have to lose some battles in order to win the war.** I had a few bad bosses. Sometimes, I figured how to get out of their departments. The way to do that was to make them look good, to do a really good job and convince them they would look better to promote me out of their departments."

Alex Sink, former chief financial officer for the State of Florida, once the most powerful woman in American banking

"My parents were my role models. They taught me about justice. **There's nothing more important than education,** that the sky was the limit, or maybe not the limit, that we could do anything we wanted to do. But, we had to be good people. Fair, decent, law-abiding. And we had to love this country."

Helen Thomas, legend of journalism

"Almost every idea that changes the status quo starts out with, 'You've got to be crazy, it will never happen.' But, **if you can last long enough, there is nothing more powerful than an idea whose time has come.** Things move from 'You're crazy' to 'We can talk about it, but it won't work' to 'I guess we'll give it a trial period, but it won't work' to having the trial period and it works well to the person in power saying 'It worked well because I proposed this idea a long time ago.' That has happened to so many women over the years. The accolades and recognition go to someone else when other people finally say, 'Why did they do it the wrong way in the first place?' "

Miriam Reed, first female division chief in the Denver Police Department, who later sued for discrimination

"Lead from behind. That's where the true leadership is. Consult with the people you are leading, listen to them and categorize their opinions. **In true leadership, you wait until everybody else has spoken. If what you say is all you, you are doing it all wrong.** True leadership comes from directing and example. You should only be a directional operator."

Betty Williams, winner of the Nobel Peace Prize for starting the non-violence movement in Northern Ireland

"My big problem is keeping myself from crying. I fail more than I succeed. **When I get mad, I cry. We lose dignity when we do that.** People expect us to be stronger than that. My mother thinks it is so terrible— a good girl doesn't cry because you don't impose your feelings on other people."

Cokie Roberts, ABC News

"The country I love will cease to be if people can't speak out and ask questions. Then the real damage will have been done. I don't think the United States would miss me if I never did another movie. **I could find lots of other things that would make me feel whole and bring joy into my life.** But, to have this country lose its civil liberties? That would be tragic."

Susan Sarandon, Academy Award-winning actress

"What you are is God's gift to you. **What you make of yourself is your gift to God.** You have a choice. Recognizing that the choice is always yours is important. Having self-possession and self-awareness is important. And, having the self-confidence to try enough different things that you really learn who you are and what you are capable of is important. That requires risk. It can't be done without risk or mistakes."

Carly Fiorina, former CEO, Hewlett-Packard

"The biggest challenge in my life has been to try to continue with my life and my work while dealing with an unbelievable array of health issues. I've dealt with that the same way I dealt with the opposition I had because I was a woman. **It's a problem, I acknowledge it and I try to deal with it the best way I know how, and then move on.** Just like I don't let my energy be siphoned off into questions of whether women should be in leadership, I won't let my energy be siphoned off by a question of health. I can control my mind when I don't control my body. I can do what I can to keep myself well and continue on. It's really a choice. You can dwell on hard or bad things if you want. You don't have to."

The late Wilma Mankiller, first woman chief of the Cherokee Nation, who faced unbelievable adversity, surviving a car accident that forced her to undergo dozens of operations, a neuromuscular disease and a kidney transplant

"It's very important for you to look within yourself at what your biases are. What buttons are pushed, and why they are pushed? **What are you doing in your everyday life to help disabled people to come into the community?** Do you look for disabled people to hire? Do you view the issues affecting disabled people the same way they feel about the issues affecting other minorities? Do you even see us as a minority? Do you feel vulnerable because you could become like us?"

Judith Heumann, special advisor on disability rights for the U.S. State Department in the Obama Administration

"**The first necessity is to find a club of 'Good Old Women.'** This will be an important step to avoid the monopoly of power. We did it. We made progress in that. Men had places where they met—the military, sports clubs—and it was a one-gender society. We had many opportunities to work together. There was more networking than mentoring. Mentoring is in vogue now that we have women in responsible positions. The first generation has to network."

Ruth Dreifuss, former president of Switzerland

"I don't think men deal with losing very well. When they aren't able to achieve the level they want to achieve, it haunts them for a long time. Women move on or find another way to get where we are trying to go. When I play a man, I don't try to strip his male pride. I want him to know that we, as women, are capable of beating men, but it doesn't have to be a male-female thing. It can just be between me, Teresa, and whoever else it is. **I say jokingly, 'I'll make sure to leave you with your manhood. But I am going to win this game.'** Our bodies and our minds are different. That's been proven time and time again. Strength is not in the size of your muscles. I think God made men stronger physically. I agree with that. I don't think I should get in the weight room and try to be stronger than a man. I should get in the weight room and be as strong as I can be."

Teresa Edwards, women's basketball legend and four-time Olympic gold medalist

"My picture in my dressing room at a comedy club was defaced with graffiti that said I'm fat and I'm not funny. Nothing had been written on anybody else's picture, and there weren't many women's pictures in there. Now I know to deflect it. The real strength is not ignoring something like that. **It's standing up and saying, 'This is not acceptable.'** I've learned to do that now, but before, I didn't want to appear bothered by it or weak. I told the club managers that if the photograph wasn't removed, I wasn't performing. I said I wasn't going on stage and they'd have to tell the audience and refund all the money. It was a sold-out crowd. Within the hour, all the graffiti was painted over."

Comedienne **Margaret Cho**

"Just concentrate on what you have to get done, and the nerves will dissipate. **Would you rather be somewhere else? Not really. This is what you have worked for, what you've practiced for.** When I am in a tournament, I worked my ass off to get there. That is where I want to be. I want to be there, not on some beach in Acapulco. And, if you don't want to be where you are, you are in the wrong line of work."

Tennis legend **Martina Navratilova**

"I have my worry rule. If you need to worry, **sit down for 15 minutes and really worry.** Then say, 'Okay. I did my worrying for today. Now let's get on with it."

Sally Priesand, the first woman ordained as a rabbi in this country

"When I know it is the right thing, I have always tried to trust my instincts. People may say, 'You can't do that.' Well, why? You have to just blow off the naysayers who insist that what you are doing is impossible. Have ten minutes of angst about it, go home, call them every name in the book, complain to your nearest and dearest about how stupid everyone is, get it out of your system, then go on. **There is absolutely no value added to stewing over the negative things people say to you.** That, I've learned."

Ann Rubenstein Tisch philanthropist, and founder of the Young Women's Leadership School

"People are going to impugn your motives for a lot of reasons. The most important thing to remember is to **always make an effort to reach out to people and explain why it is you are doing what you are doing,** rather than just closing down and feeling they are all after you because you are a woman or this is a dog-eat-dog world. That's the biggest mistake."

Christine Todd Whitman, former Environmental Protection Agency administrator and former New Jersey governor

"I've learned that **everything I think I am seeing isn't real.** There is always more than meets the eye."

Brett Butler, actress and comedienne

"In a work environment where you are a manager or a leader, a lot of people may be directing barbs that are not directed at you, but at 'the leader' who is that impersonal person who is making unpopular decisions. You have to get a tough skin on the outside, even though on the inside you care about people. **Act on your emotions and feelings from an ethical place that is consistent.** You have to learn that early on, or you will get caught in crossfires, conundrums, or hurt feelings. Once you feel hurt and can't trust people, you can't be an effective leader. If you start to withdraw, you can't be effective."

Yolanda Moses, former president of the American Association for Higher Education and the former president of City College of New York

"I saw very little of Margaret Thatcher over the years. She wasn't a woman who had much to do with other women politicians. And, unfortunately, she had very little sense of humor. She wasn't someone you tended to get in conversation with. All of those years, she had just one woman in her cabinet, and there were women of her own party who were equal to the men she had appointed—in fact, in some cases, better. **I can't decide whether she didn't think other women could do what she had done or whether she just didn't want the competition.** Most of us felt she didn't want the competition. There was a lesson in that."

Margaret Beckett, former British Foreign Secretary and former head of the British House of Commons

"Even in the hardest times, I've never said, 'I don't want to do this anymore.' I know if I say something like that to myself, it will go into a downward spiral. So, I ask myself, **'How do I get through this?** Am I going to just get through this and just maintain or am I going to get through this and go well beyond?'"

Ret. Gen. Claudia Kennedy, the first woman three-star general in the U.S. Army

"People tell me I look good these days. I look good because I feel good. I know people who are older than I am who are twenty-five. I just came up from the gym an hour ago. I work out. I think it's important. I don't dance much in my big concert shows anymore because my knees are shot. **It's all about attitude.** To me, age is just a number."

Rita Moreno, Actress

"I make mistakes every day, but it's a lot like skiing. **To get better, you have to wipe out.** If you don't, you are never going to get better, and you are not pushing yourself. You have to break down to break through."

Betsy Bernard, former president of AT&T

"Women should be very concerned about their business reputation—how they speak, how they conduct themselves, what kind of language they use, and their aggressive tactics. **All of those things can be misinterpreted.** Men can be misinterpreted also, but women more so. Their business conduct can send a very wonderful message about them as women and as executives. Every time you have an interaction with a colleague, with your boss, with someone outside your company, you have to realize that you're constantly making an impression, whether it's the first time or the twentieth."

Janet L. Robinson, New York Times CEO

"If you encounter criticism, just remember **people don't take time to get you straightened out unless you are worth straightening out.** So, when you get criticized, you have to remember someone thinks you are worth assisting."

Ret. Gen. Claudia Kennedy, the first woman three-star general in the U.S. Army

"Don't ask? Don't get. **What's the worst thing somebody could say?** The one thing you know for sure is if you don't ask, you're not going to get it for sure."

Betsy Bernard, former AT&T president

"There are always detractors. Someone will tell you you're too short to play basketball, too dumb to be a lawyer. You have to go home and say, 'Is there any truth to that?' **You have to process all the information and then decide how much weight you are going to give to your critics.** One of the things you learn to do is hear the criticism, try not to be defensive or counterattack, then go back home where it is quiet and pull the criticism out and say, 'How much validity is there to this? Should I take it to heart?' If you can learn to delay that, you won't distort everything in your head."

Dr. Nancy Dickey, first woman president of the American Medical Association

"Anybody who is criticized feels sore about it. **I don't know if it is worse if it is true or untrue.** Either criticism hurts. But my motto has always been, 'Don't let the bastards know they have gotten to you.'"

Margaret Beckett, former British Foreign Secretary and former head of the British House of Commons

"If you ask people for something, **it often makes them happy to do things, and then they are allowed to ask for something in return.** One of the great things about being successful is that you can do something for someone else."

Eve Ensler, acclaimed playwright and author of The Vagina Monologues.

"You have to get past that voice that says you shouldn't ask for things, because asking is taking advantage of people. **People ask me, and I'm glad to give them help,** usually. It's something I like to do."

Comedienne and actress **Sandra Bernhard**

"I had a great mentor. He was a man, and years ago he told me, **'You don't have to conform, Marie. You just have to look like it**.' He had a crew cut, but he was the most radical man I have ever met. Until the world changes and it is safer to be a strong, shit-kicking woman, we need to figure out how to understand the culture and move in a way we can get things done."

Marie Wilson, president of The White House Project and former president of the Ms. Foundation

"You can't get anything done without people helping you, and the only way they can help you is if you ask for it. My experience has been that when you ask for help, people are so pleased and so flattered that someone cares about their opinion and stature that they are thrilled to give it… What women have not learned is that **the worst thing that can happen to them is the other person can say no.** In that case, you just go to the next person on the list and ask them."

The late, legendary Texas Governor **Ann Richards**

"I still get intimidated by bigger-than-life, famous people. Oprah was our keynote speaker for our first graduation. I was totally intimidated by Oprah. My God, it's Oprah Winfrey and I am just little Ann Rubenstein [Tisch] from Kansas City! But, when you are intimidated, fake it. **For the five-minute conversation, or the letter you are going to write, or the meeting you are going to attend, just fake it. Put yourself right on their level. You can collapse later.**"

Ann Rubenstein Tisch, philanthropist, founder of the Young Women's Leadership School

"Have an idea about where you want to wind up, because normally the people in charge don't have a plan for you. You could very well wind up some place accidentally that you never wanted to be, not because they have an evil plan for you but because they are thinking about other stuff and you sort of fit into the slot right then. **You have to have your own vision.** Don't presume that anybody else is going to figure out where you ought to be."

Gail Collins, New York Times columnist and former editorial page editor for the Times

"We can have an overdeveloped sense of humility that causes us not to take advantage of our influence or power. Power is the ability to create change through your personal influence. I'm not sure I could even describe what power was during the first decade of my career, even though I used it unconsciously. **You use the influence you have wherever you are.** You use influence to get things done, you use your network to get things done, and then it gets to the point where you have enough of it that you decide whether or not you have a responsibility to use it for good on a larger stage. That is a conscious decision people make. I do have a significant amount of power and influence, and I not only felt an obligation to use it, but to use it for good."

Betsy Bernard, while she was president of AT&T

"In the old days, when women talked about power, it was unfeminine, aggressive, masculine. Those were characteristics that set people on edge, made them worry and made them concerned. **Now women understand that power is all about the ability to effect change.** To get anything done, you have to have some power."

Christine Todd Whitman, former head of the Environmental Protection Agency and former New Jersey governor

"You don't have any power if you don't use it. What is power if it is not used? It is a meaningless concept. **If someone is unwilling to exert power, they have no power.** Power is not something that is out there. It is something you say, 'I will use this to obtain what I want.' Other people know if you are going to fight. If they know you won't, you have no power."

Dr. Alexa Canady, first African-American woman to become a neurosurgeon.

"Sobriety has taught me that, **if there is a trait in someone else that I do not like, many times, it is a trait in myself** that I have neglected to work on."

Brett Butler, Comedienne and actress

"They felt no black woman from Arkansas could ever be qualified to be the surgeon general. Most people didn't even know that I was a doctor. They'd call me 'Miss Elders.' They figured the best I could be was a nurse. But I am a pediatric endocrinologist. There weren't many doctors around that had more training than I did. **People are ignorant. They don't have enough knowledge and they criticize you. Why get upset with someone who is ignorant?**"

Joycelyn Elders, former U.S. surgeon general

"The things that I have accomplished in my life—the ones that I believe are the most important—are the ones that were the most difficult to achieve and the most controversial at the time. **The most important things that I have done that were lasting and had purpose were not always done easily.** They were often subject to criticism and were often things that one of fainter spirit would have walked away from. But that is not so unusual. Change does not come easily."

Dr. Bernadine Healy, former director of the National Institutes of Health and president and CEO of the American Red Cross

"People are longing for leadership. **Leadership for me is about looking around the corner and seeing the crises that are imminent and dealing with them before the Titanic hits the iceberg.** For me, that's a great quality of leadership. It's also being able to carry the people with you. You have to carry a critical mass with you to get things done. You need to communicate. Be clear about what you are communicating, and don't take things personally when you encounter resistance."

Arianna Huffington, columnist, author, founder of
The Huffington Post

"Average people are always going to try to pull you down because **excellence is intimidating to them.** Their comfort is threatened. You have to decide if you are out here to be liked, or to be all you can be."

Legendary educator **Marva Collins**

"You make mistakes, but that's life. Don't get discouraged. **We have an incredibly forgiving society.** People have second chances all the time."

Elaine Chao, former U.S. Secretary of Labor

"When I hear criticism, I ask myself if this is my problem or someone else's. If it's mine, of course it needs to be dealt with. But if it is someone else who is trying to undermine me or the fact that a woman leader exists, then I try to put it away. **People will often say things to distract you.** You need to differentiate between those that are genuine and need addressing, and those that are cheap and shallow attempts to say you aren't capable of dealing with your responsibility."

Jenny Shipley, former prime minister of New Zealand

"I would get someone to prep me on what was going on in sports, because almost all meetings with men begin with what is going on in sports. Whether Sammy Sosa hit another home run or Michael Jordan is really going to retire again, **you need to be slightly conversant with that world.** You don't have to know a lot. Just enough to know what they are talking about. Know how to make a contact. You have to learn to talk about the weather and what's playing at the theater because most people, when they get together, do not go directly to the business at hand. There is a lot of foreplay."

Ann Richards, The late, legendary Texas governor

"I put it down to envy. I think people who worry a lot about someone else who got something that they didn't are not attending to the right things. It's really none of their business. **It's really just their business to be as good as they can be and stop worrying about the person on the left or right** in terms of competing with them. What we really should be doing is competing with our own personal best—not competing with a peer."

Ret. Gen. Claudia Kennedy, the first woman three-star general in the U.S. Army

"Life now is so rush, rush, rush. It's not workable to rush, rush, rush—hoping life will suddenly be peaceful and nice. Instead, we need to look at the choices we are making by asking these questions: **What do I value? My health? My sanity?** Being with my family and having my kids feel nurtured and loved? What? Are another car and big wages more important?"

Spiritual teacher **Brooke Medicine Eagle**

"Don't be timid about your power. Use it. Risk disapproval. The most important thing is that you know life goes on, and no one conflict is going to ruin you. I am criticized for being aggressive, being driven—**characteristics that nobody questions in a man but constantly questions in a woman.** It is important that women who have the passion to lead are able to do that without holding back. If you have this burning desire to change things and make a difference, don't hold back. We all have different destinies."

Arianna Huffington, columnist, author, founder of The Huffington Post

"**I'm very threatening to people. So be it.** I try not to throw that up in people's faces."

Carly Fiorina, former CEO of Hewlett-Packard

"You do learn from things. Then you have to go on and do something else. **I feel most sorry for the women who get trapped and can't get beyond the victim stage.** If you stay there, you're victimizing yourself. You're going to be there forever. What's the point of that?"

Penny Harrington, first woman chief of a major metropolitan police department

"When I was born, I was always told I was the best baby born in the world. I was nurtured by my parents, grandparents, aunts, uncles and all their associates. When we went to my mother's church, they wouldn't ask if I was going to college, it was, 'Where are you going to college?' Then they'd put five dollars in my hand and say, 'You go there and do well. You need to be class valedictorian.' I thought, **'Dang, I need to do well.'** I went to college with the confidence that they knew I would succeed."

Rev. Suzan Johnson Cook, author, pastor and U.S. Ambassador-at-Large for International Religious Freedom

"There isn't anybody who isn't going to have ups and downs. I call them 'course corrections.' All of us have had mountaintop experiences, but you don't ever stay on the mountaintop. **At some point, you are going to end up back in the valley,** either voluntarily or involuntarily."

Sarah Weddington, the attorney who won the landmark 1973 Roe v. Wade case in front of the U.S. Supreme Court.

"I've had periods of achievement and other periods that weren't particularly great. For a while there, I was thinking I was setting up a pattern of making some huge mistake I'd need to recover from every two years. Sometimes I have to say, **'Look, stop struggling so hard.** Just do some minimums for a while. Get through this bad period.' "

Ret. Gen. Claudia Kennedy, the first woman three-star general in the U.S. Army

"The moral to this story is, take responsibility for your own health. Listen to your own body. **Don't be intimidated by other people telling you that you are wrong.** In more cases than I can count, doctors have said, 'Oh, it's nothing,' and it ends up being cancer. Get other opinions. Most people know what their body normally feels like.

Today, I woke up at the beach and it was overcast and foggy—really eastern kind of weather, and I took a walk and it was just wonderful. **It is important to seize wonderful moments as they happen.** Recognize when people are nice to you or recognize that something is particularly pretty or know when something makes you smile. If that can happen once or twice a day, you have it made."

Mary-Ellis Bunim, the late creator of MTV's Real World, pioneer of reality television who valiantly fought breast cancer until her death in 2004

"I have seen many very talented people really do damage to their careers because they were **so focused on the next thing** that they didn't spend the time or attention they needed on the current thing."

Carly Fiorina, former CEO of Hewlett-Packard

"We know the meaning of life. It is not a $50 million contract for seven years. That's not the meaning of life. The hardest thing to teach is that **peace of mind is so much more important than the biggest bank account.** You have to be the best you can possibly be on this earth, and you have to grow as a person."

Teresa Edwards, women's basketball legend

"I think many women are tired. Many of us are trailblazing into industries that are traditionally male. The culture is still male and when you go to a day's work, you then come home and have to have time for family. You look around for time for yourself and you've given out all of your 'oomph.' Your strength is gone. It is very difficult to prioritize and focus when you are burned out.

When you feel tired you make wrong decisions, bad decisions, decisions that aren't right for you. You are too tired to think clearly. **Find time for yourself.** If that means instead of taking a lunch break you go to a park and take a 'me break,' do it. Find whatever amount of time you have that no one else can capture."

Rev. Suzan Johnson Cook, author, pastor and U.S. Ambassador-at-Large for International Religious Freedom

"I was once in Florida with my mother, when I got a call from my daughter Elizabeth. She ended her one very long sentence by saying 'There is a fire in the Oakland hills and we have to evacuate in twenty minutes, what should I take?' **You start to rank things in importance.** It's, 'Get out of there as fast as you can. If you can, take the animals, and maybe the photographs.' My many books, that would be a great loss. My plants, they are irreplaceable. But the main thing is life. The winds favored us in that fire. Others lost, but we survived. It sharpened our focus. What matters is life."

Oceanographer **Sylvia Earle**, "Her Deepness"

"We have not had culturally approved ways to deal with other women except as rivals for a limited supply of the goodies or men. But most of it is our internalized distrust of other women. It comes from the zero-sum model that says there is only so much to go around, and if I take mine, there will be less for you. It also comes from valuing men over women. **Women are taught from the earliest age to jockey for position instead of seeing the value of their relationships with women.** I'm thrilled we are finally shedding light on this dark area. It is time. Women are never going to get anywhere as a gender and reach equality with men if we are still fighting with one another."

Dr. Christiane Northrup, best-selling author

"The reason I push women to get out to walk or run
is that they then take ten or twenty or thirty minutes
a day and have a window of time to **get things clear
and focused**. You also get an endorphin rush from
exercise. Most women have never had that before.
That allows them to feel positive about something.
If you feel positive, you have a sense of hope. If you
have hope, you can have courage."

Kathrine Switzer, the first woman to officially run the Boston
Marathon

"Often, we have patterns set up that say 'Compete. You'll never get anything in life unless you push somebody else down and get on top of them.' Someone else has to lose in order for you to have what you need. This is the opposite of the truth that **we are all in this together**, and that helping each other is how we all can create an abundant, sustaining and happy life. It's certainly not by damaging people or by hurting or competing with one another."

Spiritual teacher **Brooke Medicine Eagle**

"When I wrote the first book, I thought I would lose my license. It was terrifying. I had this moment, a wall of fear I had to walk through. That was the night before my hospital grand rounds meeting—the first time I faced my colleagues since writing the book. What would they say? What happened was exactly nothing. Nobody cared! They were all living their own lives, going about their own business. Did they talk about me in the operating room? Absolutely. **Like most women, I had to get over my fear of not being liked.** That is huge for most women, and it was huge for me. But I didn't get killed."

Dr. Christiane Northrup, on what she expected when her revolutionary women's health book, Women's Bodies, Women's Wisdom, was published.

"I know how to use toughness when I need to. I don't expect to be liked. I've had only female chiefs of staff, and they would visibly cringe when somebody didn't like them. I'd say, **'Why do you expect them all to like you? Do you like everybody?'** Some people see me as a bitch, but it is okay to be seen as a bitch. Then they don't step on you as much."

Loretta Lynch, the famed lightning rod who headed California's Public Utilities Commission

"I learned quickly in my career that you have to be able to say you made a mistake. If you are speaking with a person who is very upset about something, it is easier to say, 'I'm sorry, I was wrong.' You take the wind out of their sails. You can move forward and figure out how to fix it. It shows you care. You're not afraid to say you made a mistake and you are willing to listen."

Rabbi Sally Priesand, the first woman ordained as a rabbi

"If I had to choose between the two months of the expedition and the one day of the summit, I would choose the two months. It's about relationships. Life is easier than we make it out to be. You are up there on Everest for two months with a drum of your stuff, and you are happy. You come back home and you have light you can turn on and off, a tub with water, a bathroom, a machine to clean your clothes. And you worry about your car because it has a scratch. You think about that all day and, oh, you forgot the laundry and you forgot the bread. Some people have a bad day just for that. **Why worry? Look at all the things we have and be happy.** I can be happy just sitting on a mountain."

Araceli Segarra, who climbed Mount Everest with the IMAX team

"No matter how much progress we have made toward equitably sharing roles, at least for my lifetime, it looks like women still carry more than their share in the vast majority of cases. Seriously. I don't sleep eight hours a night. **I sleep more like five or six hours so I have two to four extra hours to do things. And I couldn't have possibly done what I've done without a supportive spouse.** Middle age is telling me you can't do everything all at one time."

Dr. Nancy Dickey, first woman president of the American Medical Association

"The idea that anybody can do it all is preposterous. Yet, despite all the beliefs that a lot of modern marriages are egalitarian and have the assumption of shared child care and domestic efforts, **women still do the majority, if not the totality, of the domestic side of work.** Even if they are working fifty, sixty, seventy hours a week at a job, women still seem to bear the brunt of the burden. They are also supposed to be great moms, great hostesses, have the perfect house, perfect meals, perfect children, perfect hairdo and perfect whatever. I don't think that has changed."

Maryanne LaFrance, Yale psychology professor

"When I went to Congress in 1972, reporters asked me what I feared most. I said, 'Losing my housekeeper.' Editorials slammed me for being so petty. They wanted me to say something very profound, like what I feared most was not being able to move a major bill in my first term. Hell, that's easy. That was a piece of cake. They didn't understand. I would say, 'There is no member of Congress who is in the jeopardy I'm in if my housekeeper leaves. If my housekeeper leaves, my life stops.' "

Patricia Schroeder, the legendary, former U.S. Congress-woman

"You have to know when to conform and when to go along, versus when to shake the tree and pick a battle. **There are many, many things you see going on that you don't agree with. You just have to bite your tongue and say, 'This is not my battle.** I'm going to speak up when I see something I'm very convinced about, something I am passionate about.' But it can't be every time because, eventually, you'll get a reputation as being a negative someone who won't go along, won't fit in—somebody who is a troublemaker."

Alex Sink, former chief financial officer for the state of Florida and once the most powerful woman in American banking

"I will never forget the day when my son was a senior in high school and he asked me if I would be traveling on a certain day because a couple of coaches wanted to talk to me about a college scholarship. It blew me away. College? I hadn't even thought about it. **I wasn't living in the present. I was so intensely holding on to whatever it was, keeping all the balls up in the air.** Then it dawned on me, this kid is leaving. I became a much better parent."

Gayle Greer, former senior vice president, Time-Warner Cable

"I'm often asked how I do so much at once. The way you do it is you recognize that having children is a partnership with more than one person. We all have families in one form or another, by blood or closeness. If we only looked at ourselves as part of a bigger unit, it wouldn't be so intimidating to have children. **Children benefit from having different caretakers, different parents.** It's not just a relationship between a father and mother. Instead of thinking it is all the responsibility of one person— usually the mother—realize it's a responsibility and a joy to be shared by all. I am actually encouraged as I meet a lot of women juggling families and careers who are taking turns with others. There are many more stories about househusbands, men who work at home or stay home with the children. There is more openness about discussing the possibilities. People are less tied to the old, rigid roles."

Aida Alvarez, former head of the Small Business Administration

"A man is described as 'tough' and that is acclaimed. When a woman is described as tough, that is a nasty thing to say about her. And, what do you mean by 'tough'? Tough-mean or tough-minded? Leadership is about being tough-minded, compassionate and tough-minded. **Tough criticism is a gift** because it forces you to re-examine something you are doing. The world is filled with people who are different types. But I think the women who tend to get to the top are the ones on the feistier side, willing to stand up, take the heat, and fight for what they believe is right. They are welcoming of healthy debate. I just think that's the way life should be."

Dr. Bernadine Healy, former director of the National Institutes of Health and president and CEO of the American Red Cross

"What do people expect of me? 'Janet, you've got to get smaller glasses.' 'Janet, you've got to get larger glasses.' 'Janet, you've got to get different colored glasses.' 'Janet, you looked perfectly smashing on Good Morning America today.' I'll say, **'Thank you. What did I say?'** and they'll say, 'Uh, I didn't pay attention.' "

Janet Reno, former U.S. Attorney General

"Our sex is the single most important factor that triggers how people react to us. The assumption is that men are competent and women are not. **Women have to prove they are competent.** Men do not."

Kim Campbell, Former Canadian Prime Minister

"Controlled chaos is easier than spontaneous chaos for me. I just finished a play that I did seven days a week that included a half-hour monologue, a bunch of rolling on the floor and throwing myself around the stage. That was a breeze. Whereas Sunday I had a bowling party for my son's fifth birthday. I needed Valium. I was begging someone for it. I had a glass of wine at four in the afternoon."

Frances McDormand, Academy Award-winning actress

"Take a small step. It always, always makes a difference. Too many decisions are made by default by those who choose not to take that small step to protect the things they love. They leave it to somebody else, assuming somebody else is looking out for clean water, for the education of their children, or whatever the issue is that they care about. But you can't count on anybody else being out there to take up your slack.

If you don't do or say anything, then you are part of the problem. If you, in your heart, disagree and just go along without saying anything, you are speaking through your silence. Your voice is silent, and others are speaking for you."

Oceanographer **Sylvia Earle**, "Her Deepness"

"When my children were smaller, we had a family diary and if they wanted to do something, they wrote it in the diary. **Each Sunday, the family would sit down and we would talk about what I had to do and what they needed to do.** Everyone was respectful of each other's needs. It wasn't always Mum who would do it. It might be Burton, it might be Granny, but it still saw that the needs of the children were met and recognized."

Jenny Shipley, former prime minister of New Zealand

"First of all, a lot of whistleblowers get fired. That shuts them up in a hurry because they have to find a job. And they can't complain too much about their former employer when they are trying to figure out how to pay their own mortgages. Still, sometimes, there is no other choice. **At the end of your life, you have to know you stood for what is right.** Your only choice is to tell the truth."

Enron Whistleblower **Sherron Watkins**

"The times I am quickest to judge and dislike are the times, lately, when I have been pulling myself closer and looking at what is lovable about the unlovable, what is sane in the nuts. I live in Los Angeles and I see a woman who is surgically mutilated behind the tinted windows of a $150,000 car, and she looks like such a stuck-up bitch. I look closer, and **I see a scared little chick.**"

Comedienne and actress **Brett Butler**

"Nobody in my family ever told us that there were things we couldn't do because we were female, or things we couldn't do because we were poor or things we couldn't do because we were Native American. We didn't feel there were limits on what we could do. The single most important lesson I learned by watching people in my community is that **it is important to have a good attitude and keep your mind free of negative thoughts.** I saw people facing the most daunting sense of personal or financial problems, yet they always found something positive in their situation. They looked at the positive, rather than the negative. That's important. It's your choice."

Wilma Mankiller, first woman to lead the Cherokee Nation as principal chief

"I have a job, I have friends, I have church, I have family. **If one goes wrong, I kick it to the curb** so my energy goes to those other things. Your life is made up of so many things. Struggle in one area doesn't reflect your performance in the others."

Jane Smith, former CEO of Business and Professional Women USA

"I remember what my dad said when I called to tell him I'd made one star. He let out a yell, then he said, **'OK, celebrate tonight. Tomorrow morning get working on that second star.'** Pushy, pushy, pushy. There were no women two-stars."

Ret. Gen. Claudia Kennedy, first woman three-star general in the U.S. Army

"Age? So, it limits you a little bit. But I'm still a hell of a lot better playing tennis than most people in the world. Maybe not as good as I used to be, but does that mean I should not do it at all? I'm still finding new ways to hit the ball. What does it say when I beat somebody who is 23? It says I am one hell of a tennis player. Not that they aren't good, but that I am. I'm still me. That is the double standard. Yeah, I would like to be prettier, sexier. But that stuff is so inconsequential. **I'd rather be who I am and what I am on the inside than be some fake image that is gorgeous,** Yeah, I'd have liked to have been a little taller, with a smaller nose and bigger boobs, but I'm not going to have surgery. I don't mean to sound egotistical. I like who I am."

Tennis legend **Martina Navratilova**

"The four visions my mom left me are, 'Always do your best, that's good enough'; 'Never throw away your tomorrows worrying about yesterday'; **'The day you see the truth and cease to speak is the day you die'**; and 'If you want to get out of the cotton patch, you have to get something in your head.' "

Dr. Joycelyn Elders, former U.S. surgeon general

"I learned a long time ago that you just have to ask what you don't know. **So when I got here, I asked a lot of questions.** I'm sure a lot of technology executives thought, God, she doesn't know a lot, but when you ask, they want to help you understand."

Meg Whitman, the CEO who turned eBay into a way of life

"People who are brave are scared. If they weren't scared, they wouldn't need to be brave. When you take a risk, you can fail. I don't care how successful you are. You feel that. I feel that every day… **But if you don't make mistakes, you are not taking risks.** If you are not taking risks, you are not learning."

Aida Alvarez, former head of the Small Business Administration

"It's often assumed that people who find themselves taking some kind of moral stand have some comfort with that decision and feel courageous and empowered. **It's only in hindsight, if it works out, that you are assessed as being brave.** While it's happening, that's not the case. But, what motivates you is the thought of having to live, knowing you were complicit by saying nothing."

Susan Sarandon, Academy Award-winning Actress

"I think people make a very big mistake by not showing their human sides. More often than not, **if people can see the sensitive side of women in business, they relate better to them.** They realize we have frailties just like they do, and it really strengthens relationships."

Janet L. Robinson, New York Times CEO, on leaving her career as an elementary school teacher behind

"Let's not pretend that the door doesn't need a little assistance **for those coming behind us.** I have the power and influence to do that, and I'd be really remiss and guilt-ridden if I didn't do that."

Betsy Bernard, former president of AT&T

"We all hear that women make 74, 75, 76 cents to a man's dollar. I used to say, 'That's a problem we ought to fight, but it's also a problem of timing. With all these women in the pipeline—young women getting into the workforce—we'll have enough women choosing to postpone childbearing. We'll have more women on the same level. This will work itself out.' Unfortunately, it hasn't."

Hillary Clinton

"One of the most shocking days I ever had was going to the first class of graduating women at the Air Force Academy. They just lit into me. They didn't know what the hell I was talking about, because they'd never been discriminated against. If any of those women had been born even a year earlier, they wouldn't have even been allowed to attend the Academy. We wouldn't have the vote if it hadn't been for a lot of women going and chaining themselves to the White House in their lovely white dresses. Women were the first to picket the White House. Our foremothers would say, **'We did all of this and you won't risk speaking up about day care?'** "

Patricia Schroeder, legendary former U.S. Congresswoman

"I wonder if, in a hundred years, they'll be sitting around talking about diversity and someone will say, 'I hired a white male today.' "

Sally McDonald, development expert

"You have to make a decision in your life. **Do you want to be 'good' or do you want to have a life?** 'Good' implies being approved of and toeing the line. Living inside a box. Behaving. Having nothing. Having everybody love you—which they never do, by the way. It's the suburban world where everything is contained and lovely and you never get your hands dirty and you never live your life. You live their life."

Eve Ensler, acclaimed playwright and author of The Vagina Monologues

"We take so much for granted today and it is so easy for people to **grouse about what they don't get**. Something costs too much. They have to wait in a line. You just say, 'Imagine being a refugee.' Imagine being a woman who can't even go to a doctor because men aren't allowed to look at women and women aren't allowed to be doctors. There are ethnic cleansings going on around the world. But people get angry that someone is driving too slow or they get angry when they get held up on an airplane because there's a technical fault and they have to get off. They get angry and shout at the personnel who had nothing to do with it. Would they rather be in the air and have a crash? Is that what they want?"

Jane Goodall, anthropologist and primatologist

"Because the word 'feminist' is not easy to wear, I feel obliged to say, 'Yes, I am a feminist.' As a trade unionist, I had to fight with the same energy for equal pay. **I feel for the women who were attacked because they said they were feminists.** There are so many reasons to push for equal opportunity. You cannot just spoil half of the labor force"

Ruth Dreifuss, first woman president of Switzerland

"The restrictions that have existed for women for all of our history were shattered during my lifetime. Nobody has a baby girl and says, 'Too bad she won't be able to do x, y, or z.' **For that to change in my lifetime is such a kick to me.** Some people worry that if we celebrate where we have come that we won't be focused on where we need to go. That is obviously true, but it's crazy if you can't sit back and say, 'Hey, this is neat. This is good.' "

Gail Collins, New York Times columnist, former editorial page editor for the Times

"When we really have power and we exert it, others get uncomfortable. But, they are getting more used to it because we are at the tipping point. **All over the world, people are getting more accustomed to women having power** and wanting women to have power because they trust what women will do with it."

Marie Wilson, president of The White House Project, former president of the Ms. Foundation

"Your most important assets are not material things, things you put in your safe deposit box or the money you put in your bank account. It's what you have in your mind, your brain. **It's what you know, who you are, and the circle of friends and allies you build.** Houses can burn, markets can crash, accidents can happen. The things you think are most important can, in a flash, be gone. But, as long as you have your mind and people who care about you and people who you care about, you can do anything."

Oceanographer **Sylvia Earle**, "Her Deepness"

The Legacy Book

The interviews for *Hard Won Wisdom* and *Mustang Sallies* inspired and changed me on a very human level. The one thing I hadn't done was interview women who had made their mark fighting the very battles most women fight in the business world. I wanted a book that would lay out the brass tacks for succeeding in business.

I often call *The NEW Woman Rules* my legacy book because it features core advice and strategies from some of the most successful women in business of our times. Among the 52 women in the book are women from Fortune's list of the most powerful women in the world. The book was underwritten by the Network of Executive Women – NEW – which is the organization that captured my heart and soul.

I'll share some of the quotes here, but the real power of that book comes in the more than 200 success "rules" that came from the interviews. If I'd had those rules when I was working in the corporate world, I would have saved myself one heck of a wild ride. Seriously, the women I interviewed know how to maneuver office politics, career trajectories and life balance in ways I never did.

"We take everything so seriously, but we shouldn't. I used to have a boss who said, 'Let's remember: We sell toilet paper.' He was one of the great people in my life."

Barbara Hartman, former vice president, Procter & Gamble, consultant and speaker, Go Beyond LLC

"Stop overworking. I come from a good, hard-working, German farmer stock—the kind that is all about putting your head low, picking the weeds and knowing good will come your way. **I plowed my first fifteen years of soil by what I now realize was not necessarily productive overwork.** I went five years without a vacation. I could have had two months to travel the world and discover new things, but I worked. How stupid was that?"

Kim Feil, vice president, chief marketing officer, Walgreens

"It is far better to have the right strategy and less-than-perfect execution. What is a disaster is having perfect execution against the wrong strategy. The business is so dynamic; **you need strategic agility in order to compete.** You have to be willing to change your strategy. You have to have the right strategy. You can't be focused on perfect execution when you have the wrong strategy."

Meg Whitman, former CEO, eBay

"I have always felt I could jump off a high building and land on my feet. . . . I never saw that ceiling that holds people down. I thought, 'I can do it. I just have to work very hard. **I always have to work harder than the person next to me.**' I came into a country that was not my country, and if I was going to succeed, I'd always have to work harder than the person next to me."

Marie Quintana, vice president, PepsiCo

"People often ask if there were anything I'd change about what I did. I often think I would have taken the time to get a degree. I don't know that it would have gotten me any further than I got, but it was a personal goal I'd set for myself that I wanted to achieve. I know that **what I got here through experience is a hundred-fold to what I would have gained going to college.** I think the more you want to learn and grow— it is all here for you."

Pat Curran, executive vice president, Walmart. She started her career in the pet department and became one of Fortune's "50 Most Powerful Women."

"If you need a title for a clear identity, then I don't want to be tied to a title. I want to be tied to who I am. Certainly, that is about what I have done, but I don't want to be known as, 'She was the CEO of Pathmark.' **I would much rather be known as, 'She was the generous, self-confident, team-building person who made a difference in lots of people's lives.'** "

Eileen Scott, former CEO, Pathmark Stores, now chief operating officer, ICC Decision Services

You are never too high up to ask for help. Actually, you are an idiot if you don't. If people want to offer advice, listen to it. You don't have to take it."

Kathy Hopinkah Hannan, national managing partner, KPMG

"My children were ten, eight and seven when I left. It was really big news because I was CEO of Pepsi-Cola North America and I'd been on all those lists—you know, like Fortune's most powerful women list and all of that. So, when I left, I was on every morning show and in every newspaper. **I was the poster child for whether women could or couldn't have it all. I didn't want to let womanhood down;** I just wanted to spend time with my kids. . . . I never felt I wasn't there as a parent. My kids were fine, but I wanted to be with them more. I wanted time with them for me. I had three children, I was living in a different city from my husband and I didn't want to live that way. I recognized my kids were growing up, and if I didn't do something to be with them then, I would miss the opportunity totally."

Brenda Barnes, who left her job as CEO of Pepsi-Cola North America to balance her life, then returned to the workforce as CEO of Sara Lee Corporation. In 2010, she suffered a massive stroke and had to leave the business.

"Over time I've learned that, in the office, there are very few people who are going to be my confidant. Anything I say, I'd better figure is going to be repeated somehow, sometime, some way. The big thing about office politics is this: **Keep your mouth shut.** As soon as somebody opens his or her mouth to say something about somebody else, you have to shut it down by saying, 'I don't want you to have this conversation around me.' If you don't say anything, he will take your silence as agreement and the next thing you know, he is telling somebody else, 'Jeri thinks ...'"

Jeri Dunn, vice president and chief information officer, Bacardi

"Building relationships is equally important to
delivering positive results. **Networking is working.**
It is really important to develop relationships with
senior executives. You have to be mindful of how
you do it. It would be helpful to just understand
what kind of opportunities your company offers for
you to network or interact with senior executives. I
made it a point that whenever there was a project or
task force or committee, I raised my hand and said,
'I want to do that.' Doing that gives you visibility.
And visibility over time and over places gets you
recognized, and when you get recognized, you have
better opportunities to be sponsored."

Denise Morrison, CEO, Campbell's Soup Company

"I watch the men banter back and forth and have strong words to each other and take strong positions, and, when the meeting is over, they pat each other on the back and talk about going to dinner with their wives the next night. But if I do it, they become very uncomfortable and their response back to me is very abbreviated and short. They avoid me—especially if I get very excited. And they think "very excited" is if I raise my voice a little bit. They will avoid me. It drives me crazy.

I want to engage in the kind of two-way discussions that they have with each other, but I can't seem to get that done. **And if there are any harsh words, there is no dialogue going on.** I almost have to go up to them and make up. These men haven't worked with women before, and I know I am making excuses for them. But that's the reality."

Janel Haugarth, executive vice president and chief operating officer, SuperValu

"My mentors and coaches taught me to be willing to ask others for help. To **never underestimate the power within you or your team,** because it isn't until heat is applied that we know there is a whistle in the teakettle. Keep the end goal in mind at all times— that vision will encourage and strengthen you during challenging times. Seek to give your teammates the assist versus needing to be the one who scores. Remember the small things: anniversaries, special occasions, thoughtful gestures, and saying thank you."

Julie Washington, senior vice president and general manager, Jamba Juice

"When something goes terribly wrong, you can choose to be a victim or you can choose to take responsibility. **Events happen every single day. Some of them are in our control, some are not.** The only thing you can control is your response."

Betsy Hosick, general manager, Chevron

"These are some of my words of wisdom: **You can always go home. You can't always reconstruct an opportunity.** You can always have a run at it and give up later if that is necessary, but it may never come again."

Susan Ivey, chairman, president and chief executive officer, Reynolds American Inc.

"First, **be clear about who you are, what you bring to the table and what you want.** Then communicate that to all the people who need to know: to your boss, your boss's boss, and those key stakeholders who can influence your career.

Second, make sure you have a clear understanding of the expectations of every assignment. Get them all spelled out. Understand what success looks like for whatever your assignment is. "I will deliver x sales and x profit.' Get measurable answers on what success is, and make sure everybody who is going to evaluate you understands that is what you are going to deliver.

Third, make your boss your biggest supporter and advocate. It is great to have a mentor, but the greatest relationship you can have is with your immediate manager. Where women fall down is, they don't invest in that relationship. Really get to understand the individual—not just formally, but learn what makes him or her tick. How can you meet the unmet needs? How can you make your boss succeed, and therefore, how can your boss make you succeed?

Fourth, have multiple folks you can turn to for advice and coaching. **Have your own personal board of directors.** No one individual has everything. Seek out those people who have something you want to learn or something you aspire to, and develop a relationship with them."

Helayne Angelus, principal, Kalypso, former vice president at Procter & Gamble

"People think that the people on the top floor have loftier minds, are craftier individuals and better strategic thinkers. It is just the same on the top floor as downstairs. The people downstairs think we must have the answers, but the people on the top floor are doing the same thing they are: sitting in a group and coming up with ideas. **The upstairs group is just a different group of people with a little more experience.** You might think you don't belong 'up there' because you assume there is a level of thinking far above what yours is, but you are wrong."

Shelley Broader, senior vice president, Sam's Club

"Sometimes we walk away from the chance to get clarity. We don't want the criticism. And sometimes I talk to some women who don't believe corporate America is a game. It is a game. Not from a manipulation standpoint, but **there are rules you need to understand.** You need to understand what is required, and all the moves and pieces that go with it."

Beverly Grant, vice president, Procter & Gamble

"When you get derailed and think it is the end of the world, it is not. Hold your head high and know you can contribute and make things work out even better in the end. **Don't get even, get better.** That just plays in my head. I have that fighting mentality. I know my value and I am going to make myself indispensable to the organization I am in."

Judy Spires, president and CEO, Kings Super Markets

"In many meetings, I am the only woman and, in some cases, the only black person. I have always used that as an advantage. Once they hear me speak and confirm that I understand the business, they start to ask for my opinion. People see me. They are waiting. I am able to use my diversity to benefit the company. **I do see things in a different way.** I have always been comfortable in a place where there are few people like me."

Reginia Stein, vice president, Kraft Foods

"To me, feminism is not a label. It is a title I am proud to wear. Many, many women died long before I got here, giving their whole lives over so I could be able to identify myself that way. I feel I owe an unpayable debt to the women who came before me. I have a moral obligation to pay it forward."

Mavis Leno, who led the charge against gender apartheid in Afghanistan.

"I think it is hard for young people to realize that a career or life in general is not a ladder. **It is a highway with lots of off-ramps and on-ramps and turns that will take you to some really interesting places.** You may have a sense that you want to go north, but you can get there by heading east and west along the way and still get there."

Melody Justice, executive vice president, the Coca-Cola Company

"I don't see failure in my career. You could look through my life and say, 'You failed there and there and there,' but what constitutes failure? **If you take what you learned and apply it to the next challenge, is that a failure?** Failure is not an option. Just learn and grow from experience."

Cathy Green, president, Food Lion

"I talk a lot about building capability. I am a very strong proponent of the idea that we should be teaching people to fish rather than giving them fish. Unless we build capabilities in our organization, we can't replicate any of the results we are creating. I've been asked why the strategy I have laid out for Kraft is different from what we have had in the past, and the answer is that **this is about how to do it—not just what to do.** At the end of the day, execution is every bit as important as strategy."

Irene Rosenfeld, CEO, Kraft Foods

"The higher you go in an organization, the more your success is dependent upon the people in your organization. You have to bring out the best in them. **You can't make every decision.** You can't be close to every detail as your span of control expands. What you can do to make the biggest impact is hire the right team, get the right people in the right jobs, then motivate and inspire them to bring out the best in them. By connecting with people, you can drive your business results."

Michelle Buck, senior vice president, chief marketing officer, the Hershey Company

"Be aware if you are aligning yourself with a certain star. You really need to be aligned with multiple stars, particularly in a large organization that is going to continually change. Leaders are going to come and go. **The main thing you have is the strength of your reputation,** and you build on that day in and day out by the decisions you make."

Carolyn Carl, vice president, the Coca-Cola Company

"Along with my principles, I stand for results. It is all about delivering results. But what I tell people today is this: It's jacks or better for openers. If you play poker, you have to have jacks to open. You have to have results to get in the game today. But **great results just get you in the game.** It is insufficient if you want to move up the success ladder and have a high-powered career.

You need to have the right image and the right exposure. Know what you stand for, what your values are and communicate them in an authentic way. Make sure you get out there and get the exposure you need to get a broad array of people behind you, not just your immediate manager. Are you networking? Do you have a mentor? Are you making contact with people who connect with your business? What are you doing to let people know who you are and what you stand for?

"What drives me is family. I have a lot of perspective about this. I lost a baby when I was seven months pregnant. You think there is pressure in business when the numbers are down, but compared to losing a baby, work pressure is a joy ride. I had never hit a hurdle like that. It was as if my life had completely collapsed.

From that point on, it didn't matter what I faced here in the office. Nothing was even close to that pain. From that, I was able to create a distance where **I do the best I can every single day, then go home at night and sleep very well.** I have an appreciation for what real drama and crisis are. It is not here. This is business. You want to embrace the business, but you don't want it to smother you. If it becomes who you are, you have a problem."

Mary Beth West, executive vice president, Kraft Foods

"It is dangerous to get so committed to what you are doing that you stop evaluating whether you are moving in the right direction. You have an opinion about what is right. **Sometimes your opinion is right, sometimes it is not.**

Sometimes you may believe you are right and you get too entrenched in wanting whatever you are working on to be accomplished your way instead of just figuring out a way to get where you need to go. Figure out the most effective way. There are always multiple ways to solve a single problem."

Linda Dillman, senior vice president, Hewlett-Packard

"When you are afraid, you have to show confidence. **People follow people who are confident in what they are doing.** They aren't going to follow you if you are unsure, if you don't have a road map somewhere. Today, I deal with things with a lot of confidence because I have all these experiences behind me."

Maureen McGurl, president, Sutton Place HR Consulting Group, former executive vice president, the Stop & Shop Supermarket Company

"Selling is all about getting to that win-win point. I don't sell people short. **I make sure that negotiations are win-win and there is benefit for everybody.** I have to live with it. I am a firm believer in the Golden Rule.

I also am a firm believer in the saying that, 'The toes you step on today may belong to the ass you have to kiss tomorrow.'

Just look at a situation. Consider first what you have to do for the business. Second, you get people to buy into that right solution by focusing on what is important to them and what their 'win' is in the outcome. You also appeal to them for the greater good, knowing the right thing to do for the business situation at hand."

Joan Toth, president and CEO, Network of Executive Women

"Men feel they win only when others lose. I see the difference in my daughter and my sons. If you bring that into a completely male-dominated corporate culture, it is all about win-lose. But there is another way of doing things. It is hard to introduce that new philosophy when there aren't a lot of women in leadership positions.

But there is an art when working with people with a win-lose mind-set. **What I try to do is come back to the intent or the objective that has put us across the table from each other.** I really, really work hard at seeing what we are trying to achieve. There is often a second agenda or motivation at play, but if I can get it back to the original intent, the second agenda gets muted. You always have to remind yourself of what your intent is. What is your objective?"

Mary Gendron, senior vice president, the Nielsen Co.

"Women tend to want to be 100 percent sure before they do something, whether it involves a discussion or a recommendation or turning in the results of a project. **There is an over-delivery mindset. You really only have to be about 80 percent sure.** If you can let go of that over-delivery mindset and see how far your peers are taking things, you will benefit. There are ways to do more without working at 150 percent of your capacity. It's about the boundaries you want to set. Find other people with the same passion and ideas."

Carolyn Carl, vice president, the Coca-Cola Company

"I used to believe that, unless something was perfect, it was flawed. That is not true. What is important is sifting through the garbage, identifying the most important elements and delivering those. Anyone who operates as if the last 3 percent matters will 100 percent fail today. The speed of decision-making and the quantity of decisions that have to be made are so vast now. **There is no room for overdeliberation. Identify the most relevant actions and do them very well.** Have the ability to triage a business problem. Forget about the wasteful 20 percent and go after that core 80 percent that matters the most."

Kim Feil, vice president and chief marketing officer, Walgreens

"Don't be afraid to take risks. If there was ever a point in time that I said, 'No, I don't know enough, I'm not ready, I can't,' I would have missed out on the next experience. **It is all about the chain of experiences. Each one has enabled the next one.** In totality, they have given me such a rich grouping of skills that I draw from every day. You can learn whatever it is you have to learn. You find the experts and the people who are going to support you."

Marie Quintana, vice president, PepsiCo

"When I started being a manager, women didn't want to work with women. Why wouldn't you support your own gender? That was crazy to me. It is so counter-productive when that happens. **Women should get off each other's backs and get on with it.** Who are we competing against in the business world? It's men. They are the ones who have the jobs. You have to win in a pool that is more male-dominated than female-dominated."

Brenda Barnes, former CEO, Sara Lee Corporation

"I learned to meet people where they are instead of thinking they should be where I think they should be. I learned that people learn differently—not with a cookie-cutter approach. **I learned that people will go to the wall for you when they know you care.** I learned that humility is a great leadership trait. I learned that there is more power in asking a question than making a statement. I learned that simple acts like saying 'Thank you' are worth their weight in gold. I learned that people are the company's greatest asset."

Trudy Burgeois, president and CEO Center for Workforce Excellence

"You have to toot your own horn, or at least be very honest in your self-assessment. **Don't be humble to a fault.** Other people will be taking credit for things they don't do. You have to take credit for what you are accomplishing."

Kathy Hopinkah Hannan, national managing partner, KPMG

"Everybody has a different motivation, and it's personal. If you are going to manage people, you'd better **learn what motivates each individual** or you won't build an effective team."

Michelle Gloeckler, senior vice president, Walmart

"I've learned a lot about moving a career along. Sometimes you have to take a path that is nonlinear. Don't be afraid to go lateral. Sometimes lateral moves create the best experiences. They may be the biggest game changers in your career. I made a lateral move when I took over merchandising after being in operations for so many years. The experience I got was far greater than it would have been with an upward move inside operations. Most people don't like to get outside their comfort zones, but **I like to play in somebody else's sandbox every once in a while** because they have different toys."

Pat Curran, executive vice president, Walmart

"The first thing you do to influence others is listen and really understand everyone's point of view. Have a good grasp of the fact base. **You need a crystal-clear idea of what you want people to align with you on.** Be very clear about how the situation works, how it impacts them and their organization, and really have a dialogue about it to be sure that you are, again, securing alignment along the way. Not necessarily agreement, but alignment. Have clarity around the benefits of your idea and a plan of action that you want them to agree to."

Denise Morrison, CEO, Campbell's Soup Company

"I am willing to go up to a stranger and stick out my hand and say, "I haven't met you yet. My name is Bobbie O'Hare." You learn to do that over time. If you can become comfortable with doing that, you will meet a lot of really fascinating people."

Bobbie O'Hare, vice president, Johnson O'Hare Companies

"Overdeliver. Whatever you said you were going to do, do it better than other people and demonstrate you can add value in a lot of other areas. For me, succeeding for the business is a given. But what else can you do to distinguish yourself as a leader and to support the goals of the company and the organization?"

Helayne Angelus, principal, Kalypso, former vice president at Procter & Gamble

"You have to believe in yourself. You have to love what you do. You have to have that commitment and passion for what you are doing—whatever that is. **You have a core level of aptitude. Beyond that, it is passion and commitment.** It is being prepared to keep taking challenges and to keep pushing yourself. It is wanting to have new experiences and embracing change so you don't get comfortable in your own job and do the same thing for twenty years. You have to have a thirst for adventure and an attitude that makes you try new things."

Susan Ivey, chairman, president and CEO Reynolds American Inc.

"One of the biggest challenges we face in the workplace is merchandising our successes. Women tend to be humble about their results—and I am like that, too. We keep our noses to the grindstone and go about making things happen.

But that is important. Women expect that it is the responsibility of senior managers in the organization to notice their results. **But if there are men who are self-promoting their results and the women are not, who is going to get the attention?** It is something I have been coached on. I am still uncomfortable doing it."

Michelle Buck, senior vice president, chief marketing officer, the Hershey Company

"I keep telling people that they need to get over the idea that they are bragging. Bragging is embellishing things. I am asking people to simply state the facts. To tell what their results and principles are. Just communicate who you are and what you have accomplished. **That is not being a braggadocio or self-promoting. It is simply stating the facts.** Is it true? That's not bragging."

Maria Edelson, founder and president, Sales and Capability Development, LLC, former vice president of Customer Business Development, Evenflo Company

"Another lesson for women is, don't personalize. The guys don't. When you make a mistake, own up to it and move on. Women tend to want to be perfect and they ruminate about their mistakes. And they want people to like them. **When something goes wrong, own up to it.** Say, 'I screwed up. Here is what went wrong. Here is what I would do differently.' Then move on. You need a certain toughness that only comes from falling down and skinning your knee."

Lynn Marmer, group vice president, the Kroger Co.

"Life is a series of events. Some things we do well, some we don't. **If you don't admit to a mistake, then you can never get better.** If we learn from our mistakes, we get better and better and more confident."

Maureen McGurl, president of Sutton Place HR Consulting Group, former executive vice president, the Stop & Shop Supermarket Company

"If you can't get up every day and look yourself in the mirror and like what you see, it is a day wasted. You have to have integrity. **If you don't have integrity, you can't lead.**"

Denise Morrison, CEO, Campbell's Soup Company

188 | Fawn Germer

"Bad leaders create a culture that tells them what they want to hear. **Good leaders want the truth because they can fix it and capitalize on it.** If people are intimidated and afraid and worried about their jobs, they fear speaking up about something that is bad. You have to create an environment that opens this up. How are you going to fix anything if you don't know about it?"

Brenda Barnes, former CEO, Sara Lee Corporation

"I don't put on my game face. I am a unified individual. My public and private persona are all the same deal. People are watching what I am putting in my coffee, the dress I have on, if I have a crabby expression on my face. So they see if I am sending signals, positive or negative, that I intend or don't intend to send. **But I have integrated my public and private personas. It's all one person.** You waste so much energy and effort and stress if you have to change your behavior when you are alone and in public."

Shelley Broader, senior vice president, Sam's Club

"I could write a book on how everything I need to know about corporate America I learned from my children. One chapter would be, 'No—Me, Mommy.' They don't want you to do things for them. Your people, like your children, want to do it for themselves. They want to develop their own skills. You can be their coach.

Another chapter would be about recognition. They bring something to you, and what they don't want is for you to criticize it and show how it could be better. They want you to say, 'Look! How beautiful' But, in the work world, some leaders criticize. **You get more when you see that someone's efforts were complicated and they did a great job.** They want to hear that you think you couldn't have done any better.

Finally, I could call a chapter, 'Play Nice in the Sandbox.' That is all about corporate politics. I have found that there is so much value in building positive relationships across boundaries in the sandbox. **There is absolutely no place for mean-spirited behavior.** It's inappropriate. Be somebody whom others want to play with."

Kim Nelson, senior vice president, General Mills

"You need to do your absolute best work on everything you are asked to do, from the simplest assignment to the most complicated. **Every memo has your signature on it and it should be good work.** I think people make a mistake in waiting for the big project. They forget that the way to get the big project is by doing a lot of small ones very well."

Lynn Marmer, group vice president, the Kroger Co.

"A lot of people don't realize that information is power. I don't think a lot of women quite understand that. **Even if a discussion at work is 'confidential,' all information that is shared is really public.** If you are sharing information about yourself and a project that has implications, it is public and can be used to influence an outcome. If you are sharing something and there is an obligation by the listener to do something with it, it will be public."

Beverly Grant, vice president, Procter & Gamble

"People want to come to work with their minds—and hearts. A key piece of leadership is your ability to **be empathetic and authentic.** A key piece of that is your being able to keep your ego at the door."

Irene Rosenfeld, CEO, Kraft Foods

"You have to be able to adapt. If you can't, you can't handle true adversity when it strikes. **We all have our own individual journeys.** Your ability to go into a new situation and figure it out and make it work helps build those bravery muscles so when something does happen, you will have the muscles to get through it."

Luci Sheehan, sales and marketing consultant to U.S. and international companies

"I have always had to know how to adapt to change. It starts with you. You can't find the answers on the outside. **You have to know yourself, take care of yourself and find ways to validate what you do.** When you start looking for validation of who you are or of your accomplishments from people on the outside, you will always be searching for something you will never find."

Marie Quintana, vice president, PepsiCo

"Have the best people working for you. Let your brightest people take leadership roles. **My job is to listen and teach—not tell.** There is a tendency when you are the leader to think you have to give orders. But if that is what you do, then your organization will only be able to achieve what you can process. If you teach and enable them to think on their own—and sometimes that means letting them make mistakes—then the results you receive are multifold what they otherwise would be. Plus, it is a lot more fun."

Linda Dillman, senior vice president, Hewlett-Packard

"Every person I deal with is looking for certain things from me: that I am consistent, I'm honest, and I do what I say I am going to do—good and bad. Following up is incredibly important for building trust.

You don't say, 'Trust me.' You earn it. Then have a group that will take the hill for you. There have been a number of people who have come with me, no matter where I have gone. They enjoy working with my leadership, feel that I help their careers grow and that I expose them to the right people. That type of trust is earned."

Sandy Grimes, vice president, Johnson & Johnson

"How did I move my career along? I'd say, 'I have mastered the things you wanted me to do. Give me something more to do.' It's smarter than saying, 'I want a promotion. I want to move up the ladder.' I've had a lot of people do that and my response is that, 'You'd better be sure you are doing the job you've got very well before you find the next one.' But when you ask for more, you make a statement. And if the boss says, 'I don't think you can take on any more,' it's a key indicator that you need to ask what you are doing wrong. Asking for more is a smart way to get recognition. It's a different way, and it's a smart way."

Jeri Dunn, vice president and chief information officer, Bacardi

"Your work is not your entire life. Having that sense about balance has been very important as I have gone through my life. **Be very clear what your priorities are and recognize that you are going to have to make some tough choices,** whether it is going to a child's birthday party or declining a promotion or being available for aging parents, or commuting for an out-of-town promotion. If you decide to take on these complex roles of running businesses, having children and being a good spouse, you will have to make these tough decisions. Having it all comes with a lot of choices.'

Vicki Escarra, president and CEO of Feeding America, former chief customer service officer and chief marketing officer, Delta Airlines

"You always need to **take criticism, whether it is constructive or not, and you need to look at it seriously** to adjust things where you can. But you shouldn't obsess on it, and some of it you just have to disregard."

Janel Haugarth, executive vice president, chief operating officer, SuperValu

"I am a big believer in diversity—not just about race or religion—but in thought. **It is creating an environment that allows for constructive criticism and differing perspectives.** That is the ultimate in making diversity work. People who understand that get more value out of their teams. Diversity means engaging different perspectives and experiences, and bringing those differences together to produce something of value."

Mary Gendron, senior vice president, the Nielsen Co.

"People stay in situations when they shouldn't. It's the security issue. The old story that you know what you've got, and you don't know what you don't have. So many people have that fear of what they don't know. **You have to know that you are good at what you do, and believe you are good at what you do, and know you will always have something to do and you will always do a good job.** You will always have opportunities. It's the mediocrity that is the issue. Security is comfort. It is familiarity. It is easy. It is safe."

Nancy Croitoru, president/CEO, Food and Consumer Products of Canada

"I love people. I love connecting people and I love giving back. Networking was a really good fit for me. It is innate. It is in my DNA. It's who I am. I talked to a woman at one of our events who told me, 'Bobbie, I'm not good at networking.' It surprised me because she was gregarious. I said, 'You have three children?' She said, 'Yes.' I said, 'Who do you know at your children's school? Do you know the principal?' She said, 'Yes.' 'The teachers?' 'Yes.' 'The school nurse?' 'Yes.' 'The librarian?' 'Yes.' 'The janitor?' 'Uh, yes.' 'See? You do that at the school, but that's not what you are doing at work. You do that for your kids, but **you now need to do that for yourself professionally.** Networking is work.' "

Bobbie O'Hare, vice president, Johnson O'Hare Companies

"At age thirty-one, I met this man who I knew was going to be my life partner. Procter & Gamble was giving me the job I wanted, but I said, 'I have met this man whom I know I am going to marry.' They said, 'How long have you known him?' I said, 'Six weeks.' They said, 'Are you crazy?' I said, 'Perhaps.' **But you only have one life.** That part of my life was about to be fulfilled. I had to say, 'I can't take that job right now. I may be wrong. I doubt it.' So I turned it down and someone else got the job, and I was basically taken off the promotion list. Not as punishment, but because you didn't get two chances back then. I did marry my husband two years later.

The great thing was that things did change and I once again was given great roles with significant vertical career growth in P&G. The key was to achieve significant results in anticipation of change. You get one life."

Barbara Hartman, former vice president, Procter & Gamble, consultant and speaker, Go Beyond LLC

"Marketing taught me a lot about how to present myself in any environment. **Your personal brand is evident in the first seven seconds people see you and get an impression of you.** It is important to establish that right in the beginning. Your physical image, voice and delivery all impact the way you communicate with people. Your body language and your posture say a lot about you. You can change it. There are things you can look at and change. You can learn to stand up straighter, move your shoulders back and present."

Cristina Benitez, president, Lazos Latinos

"I was golfing with this guy in Baltimore and he was swinging in the weeds. I mean, swinging. It was like he was going to cut the grass with a machete. Swinging, swinging, swinging. And when he came back and was asked what he'd hit, he said, 'I got a four.' Four? It was twelve. At least eight. **That's how guys are. If something goes wrong or they get embarrassed, they can brush it off.** A woman will worry that she can never be seen after that, that everyone will remember how awful she golfed."

Kathy Hopinkah Hannan, national managing partner, KPMG

"You have to get to know your people, and that takes time. **If you are going to understand what motivates** them and be able to motivate them to get their peak performance in whatever job they are doing, **you have to know about them.** Why do they work? What do they like? What upsets them? How do they like to be managed? Do they need a lot of praise? Are they uncomfortable with a lot of praise? There are thousands of things."

Michelle Gloeckler, senior vice president, Walmart

"I don't chase the ever-elusive work-life balance. Balance implies that you will obtain a state of equilibrium or equality. I don't think that is real. I don't know anything that allows you to stand with a foot on one side and an equal foot on the other. Life is constantly changing. It's not about balance. It's about priorities."

Julie Washington, senior vice president and general manager, Jamba Juice

"Perception becomes reality in the absence of anything else. It is important to be active in your own career in understanding how you are being perceived. That means asking your employer or manager how you are doing. Find out what the perception is. Somebody once told me that exposure far outweighs actual performance. **If people are not familiar with your work or who you are, they are going to fill in the blanks themselves.** They will make assumptions. Sometimes that may be good. Sometimes it may not be good."

Carolyn Carl, vice president, the Coca-Cola Company

"It is really important to develop a personal mission statement and define your roles and goals. Remember Stephen Covey's 7 Habits? He has a chapter on how to create a mission statement and manage multiple roles and goals in your life. Reading that book changed my life. I did everything it outlined and updated it at my different life stages. It's been a real North Star for me.

My mission statement is to serve as a leader, lead a balanced life and apply ethical principles to make a significant difference. The fact that I can say that without even reading it shows that it is on the tip of my tongue. It guides me every day."

Denise Morrison, CEO, Campbell's Soup Company

"Remember that it is a small world. Don't burn bridges. I am working with people I worked with twenty years ago who I didn't see again until we resurfaced in the same spot. **Remember, you may be leaving a company today but run into those people years from now.** How will you feel if they walk in the door?"

Michelle Buck, senior vice president and chief marketing officer, the Hershey Company

"Nobody is great at everything. **But, you have to know and understand what you are good at,** and work as much as you can at what your opportunity areas are. That gives you the power to make changes."

Joan Toth, president and CEO, Network of Executive Women

"You have your moments in a job like this. The difficulties about the controversies are that you are trying to solve a dilemma with facts when, actually, it is an emotional debate. Nobody wants to hear facts. It's one side or the other. I always tackle the most difficult situations with a clear mindset that I can do anything for four hours. Like, a deposition, or testifying at the Department of Justice, or even our annual meetings. I say, 'I can do anything for four hours. This too shall pass.' "

Susan Ivey, chairman, president and chief executive officer, Reynolds American Inc., on what it is like as a point person for the tobacco industry

"When you are confronted with a new challenge, you can always look back and say, 'Okay, this other challenge really scared the heck out of me. I have a lot to lose if I blow this, but look at those other challenges. I made it past them.' **You go back to those old experiences and lean on them for comfort.**"

Nancy Croitoru, president and CEO, Food and Consumer Products of Canada

"Just get out there. I always say, every time you go into a lecture, prepare yourself to ask a question. Prepare to say your name and where you are from. "I am Cristina Benitez, I am president of Lazos Latinos and I have a book that just came out. I have a question..." It is a mini advertisement. Always be ready with the next question you can ask. That is an exercise that we all can do. It stretches us.

The other thing is, go up to everybody. Introduce yourself. Say who you are. Don't be afraid to introduce yourself to people. We are all people. It is not that I like networking events, but I can do them. I will say, 'I'll stand for this for 45 minutes and make four connections. And I will share something I can do to help each of those people.' Titles can be so obtuse when you are introduced, so I will ask, 'What was on your desk today? What did you do?' Then you find out what they are involved in. **It is important to try to really connect with somebody.** Otherwise, you are making small, small, small talk that never ends up going anywhere."

Cristina Benitez, president, Lazos Latinos

"The three pieces of advice I would have for others are, first, have high expectations for yourself and for the business. High expectations are the key to everything. Not impossible and unreachable expectations, but high ones for you. Stretch yourself. Grow. Mediocrity will sap your energy and strength, so never settle for that. Second, get with the right people. Find the right people, whether you join the right people or hire the right people. It all comes down to people. Third, remember this: Be sure you have a life outside the business. **The business will not love you back.**"

Melody Justice, executive vice president, the Coca-Cola Company

"As women, **we have to keep pushing.** I don't think we are in a position where we automatically will have diversity and representation. The glass ceiling hasn't been lifted. Everything is not fine. We have to be realistic and stay on top of it. When we set diversity as a core value, it helps raise the bar. It really is up to us to continue to focus on representation. If we stop what we are doing, we will end up with a very male-dominated organization, once again. We sure don't want that."

Sandy Grimes, vice president, Johnson & Johnson

"As you meet people in different situations, ask for cards. Write people back on e-mail, and keep those relationships active. Find a business connection. Send them updates on what you are doing. **There are so many ways to promote yourself,** but people have to have the facts."

Maria Edelson, founder and president, Sales and Capability Development, LLC, former vice president, Evenflo Company

"Count your blessings and appreciate the moment—
every single day. That is the moment of making a
sale, interacting with co-workers, cooking a meal—
whatever. **Just celebrate the moment.** When caught in
the details of life, you easily can lose sight of those
things, but you shouldn't. Life can change in an
instant."

Luci Sheehan, sales and marketing consultant to U.S. and
international companies

"Relationships come down to **finding a connection on some level.** And the people I have learned the most from are the ones who are least like me."

Mary Beth West, executive vice president, Kraft Foods

"**If it is worth doing, it is worth doing right.** I can't tell you how many times my father said that to me. But it's true. It's the foundation for everything."

Michelle Gloeckler, senior vice president, Walmart

"Things haven't changed as much as I would like. I still go into meetings and, instead of there being just one woman or one woman of color, there are one or maybe two or maybe three. There is still a lack of diversity. There are still too many blue-shirt men walking around, and **there aren't enough yellow shirts or pink shirts or coral.** But that's changing. It really is."

Reginia Stein, vice president, Kraft Foods

"My parents were so strong, and the values they taught me have pulled me through my whole life. **Work hard. Have a strong handshake. Have confidence. And courage. Do what you are afraid to do.** My parents taught me all of those things. They were my greatest mentors."

Maureen McGurl, president, Sutton Place HR Consulting Group, former executive vice president, the Stop & Shop Supermarket Company

"I don't have to slam my fist on the table. I don't have to swear. But I can say I am disappointed. Before, I was almost paralyzed by what other people thought. Once I started to try it on and demand with edge, people expected me to play in that space. **You want to be confident, you want to be strong and you want to be aggressive.** But you don't want to be over the top. Try to strike that balance. Relationships are critical to me. Before I learned that, I didn't want to do anything to hurt anyone. But I wasn't creating all the possibilities for the business because I was holding back."

Cathy Green, president, Food Lion

"Mind your intuition. That is your best mentor. It pays to develop a highly intuitive sense because you are the only one to whom you are truly accountable. You have to lay your head on your pillow at night and go to sleep. You have to face yourself in the mirror. **You have to know, every day, that you are proud of what you did.** When the point comes that you aren't happy with your work, you may have to make the hard decision to go. Listen to your gut."

Joan Toth, president and CEO, Network of Executive Women

"Have the confidence to know that you know the right thing to do. When something isn't feeling right with you, act on it. That's one of the problems we have in the business world today: **People don't trust their instincts.** Your instincts are there because of the knowledge and experience you have. You have to believe in yourself."

Judy Spires, president and CEO, Kings Super Markets

Conclusion

This has been my favorite book project because it gave me the chance to experience the wisdom of the women I'd interviewed after enough time had passed for me to read their words with new clarity and fresh eyes. Thoughts and ideas that didn't stand out a few years ago now strike me as deeply profound. Growth changes your experience and perspective, and I've been feeling that as I have edited this book.

I initially wanted to do this project because things had changed since my books were first published. Many of the women had changed jobs, left office, fallen off the front page or, in the cases of Ann Richards and Susan Butcher, passed away. The details on their bios may be different, but the power of their words is lasting.

I've been emboldened by all of these women. They've grown me up and helped me to embrace my own dreams and goals with certainty and strength. When I need a boost, I know which pages I need to re-read.

Editing this project and putting all of these great women together in one place has helped me to comprehend the immensity of the privilege I've been afforded. It has been an absolute honor to talk to so many women heroes and ask them anything I wanted. I knew I'd been given a front row seat to something very special, but now that I see what three books have led to, I am humbled by the opportunity I have had.

My first career was as an investigative reporter who took on institutions and veteran politicians and leaders. Laws were changed. Someone went to prison for life. It seemed so very important at the time.

But what you are holding is really my life's work. My journalism career gave me the experiences I needed so I knew what to ask. That career has given me the opportunity to get the answers and share them so women everywhere will feel better about themselves and dare to succeed at the highest levels.

We have come so far in my lifetime, but we have such a long way to go. Our biggest challenge is getting beyond our greatest obstacle – ourselves – and putting our self-esteem issues and fears in check so we can do everything that this great big world has for us.

Why not? It's our moment.

Meet the Author

"If you want to read a very inspiring book, read *Hard Won Wisdom*." – **Oprah Winfrey**

est-selling author Fawn Germer will energize your spirit and show you how to take your power and run with it. She teaches how to embrace obstacles and dare to stand up and lead – unleashing the possibilities that exist in life.

Fawn is a four-time Pulitzer Prize-nominated journalist who has personally interviewed famous leaders and legends for their perspectives on leadership and success. When Fawn left journalism to write her first book, it was rejected fifteen times — by every major publisher in the country. She persevered, and her book was published – the day before the Sept. 11 tragedies. She had to promote her book — and herself — in a very difficult moment. Hard Won Wisdom was buoyed by her ability to connect so well with live audiences, and soon, thousands of people had connected to her hopeful message.

Once Oprah told the world how "very inspiring" her book was, Fawn became one of the nation's most sought-after keynote speakers. Audiences love Fawn because she's been there. Up and down, winning and losing.

She has keynoted for the Harvard Business School, Cisco, Coca-Cola, Kraft, Accenture, NASA, State Farm, Pepsico, U.S. Department of Defense, Novartis, Exelon, Xerox, Genworth, Capital One, ADP, the Association for Corporate Growth, Boeing, KPMG and many, many other major corporations and associations.

This acclaimed investigative reporter has worked as a Florida correspondent for both *The Washington Post* and *U.S. News and World Report*. She has worked as a staff writer for *The Miami Herald* and *Denver's Rocky Mountain News*.

Fawn loves to hear from readers. Be sure to visit her at www.fawngermer.com and read her blog at www.hardwonwisdom.com.

Speaking Information
(727)467-0202
info@fawngermer.com